Behaving Together

Behaving Together

A teacher's guide to nurturing behaviour

Sarah Dove

Open University Press

Open University Press
McGraw Hill
8th Floor, 338 Euston Road
London
England
NW1 3BH

email: enquiries@openup.co.uk
world wide web: www.openup.co.uk

First edition published 2021

Copyright © Open International Publishing Limited, 2021

All rights reserved. Except for the quotation of short passages for the purposes of criticism and review, no part of this publication may be reproduced, stored in a retrieval system, or transmitted, in any form or by any means, electronic, mechanical, photocopying, recording or otherwise, without the prior written permission of the publisher or a licence from the Copyright Licensing Agency Limited. Details of such licences (for reprographic reproduction) may be obtained from the Copyright Licensing Agency Ltd of Saffron House, 6–10 Kirby Street, London EC1N 8TS.

A catalogue record of this book is available from the British Library

ISBN-13: 9780335249558
ISBN-10: 0335249558
eISBN: 9780335249565

Library of Congress Cataloging-in-Publication Data
CIP data applied for

Typeset by Transforma Pvt. Ltd., Chennai, India

Fictitious names of companies, products, people, characters and/or data that may be used herein (in case studies or in examples) are not intended to represent any real individual, company, product or event.

Praise page

Sarah has a wealth of experience that she has gained whilst 'walking the walk'. Her knowledge and skills have been honed from working directly with children and young people, and listening and respecting their thoughts and ideas. This book is full of practical strategies outlining collaborative approaches to supporting positive behaviours, and will be a hugely valuable resource, not only to read from end to end but also to dip into when we need some extra help to make a difference to the children we work with.

Cath Kitchen, BSc, MSc, NPQH, NLE,
CEO of The Skylark Partnership

Behaving Together' is an important book for anyone who is in a teaching or support role. Drawing on her substantial experience of working in Pupil Referral Units and Alternative Provision, Sarah Dove provides a helpful and wide-ranging overview of the factors - personal and organisational - that can affect pupils' behaviour. By viewing learners' actions within the context of a relationship, Sarah provides practical strategies where adult and child work in partnership to understand, address, change and prevent negative behaviour. A particularly effective tool which appears frequently throughout the book is the use of quadrant grids as self-evaluation tools. I recommend 'Behaving Together' to anyone who works with children and young people, whether one-to-one or in groups.

Steve Waters Founder and Director: Teach Well Alliance

In an educational landscape in which the complex matter of understanding and managing the emotions of sometimes difficult humans is reduced, by some, to the merely bureaucratic, this book feels like going into a sauna in which you can flush away the toxic legacy of the zero tolerance bigots and the 'know-nothings'. It sees the world and working with children through eyes of love rather than dehumanising them into factory outputs from whom absolute obedience is required. Its through-line is that we should seek to influence behaviour rather than to control it through "restrictions, punishment and isolation", and it is written by someone who has been one of the children she writes about and who has done the hard years in challenging classrooms. Its reserved and even delicate academic tone suits the seriousness of the undertaking: it is a quiet book from a practitioner who understands that sometimes quietly noticing things is the key to working with children whose lives cause them to struggle. And it contains hugely useful frameworks and ideas that will help you to understand the behaviour of your more challenging students. Reading it would make any mainstream teacher a better professional. I felt cleansed by it.

Phil Beadle, Teacher and Author

In 'Behaving Together' Sarah Dove has set out to tackle one of the most challenging areas of school life: behaviour. Through a series of frameworks, she gives educators a shared language and analytical tool that helps school staff see beyond behaviour to understand its cause. This book does not advocate for a punitive response to behaviour that challenges, but asks school staff to think "How can we work together to improve things?"

Sarah Dove articulates a set of highly effective steps for supporting pupils that move from focused noticing around behaviours, through understanding the reasons for escalating behaviour, to responding to the individual's needs, communicating these and working towards preventing behaviour incidents in the future. She encourages school staff to adopt a research-informed approach to helping pupils manage their own behaviour.

A series of illustrative case studies based on lived experiences that Sarah has had as a teacher and consultant, highlight the author's understanding of the issues she discusses.

Never didactic or prescriptive, 'Behaving Together' offers school leaders, teachers and support staff a set of tools that can be used to improve a school's response to behaviour that challenges.

Aileen Morrison, Headteacher, St Matthias Academy AP

Dedication

This book is dedicated to the hundreds of children I have met throughout my career and to the teachers who have found things hard, but want to do their best for the children they work with. It is also dedicated to my daughter, Octavia, who has taught me how to be a parent as well as a teacher.

My year of writing and publishing this book has been marked by loss and sadness. As the book grew, I lost family that I loved and held dear. Nearing the end of writing the book my Uncle, Andrew Hickman died suddenly. He was looking forward to reading it, so I sadly dedicate it to him – the book he was never able to read, and I was never able to share with him.

Finally, to my Grandmother, who I know as "Budde" but others as Rhoda "Rose" Lever, a women whose intellect and memory didn't fail even at the end. I miss and love you both and hope to continue to honour your memories.

Contents

Acknowledgements	xi
INTRODUCTION	1

PART I IDENTIFYING — 7
1	WHAT IS BEHAVIOUR?	9
2	IDENTIFYING: CORRELATION WITH KNOWN CONDITIONS	13

PART II UNDERSTANDING — 29
3	UNDERSTANDING	31
4	FORMULA OF UNDERSTANDING	47
5	COGNITIVE CONTRIBUTORS	54
6	PSYCHOLOGICAL FACTORS: MENTAL DISTRESS	63
7	UNDERSTANDING PSYCHOLOGICAL FACTORS: MENTAL ILLNESS	68
8	UNDERSTANDING MENTAL DIVERSITY	80
9	RECOGNIZING RELATIONSHIPS	84

PART III RESPONDING — 91
10	INDIVIDUAL PREPARATION	93
11	RESPONDING: INDIVIDUAL EXECUTION	98

PART IV COMMUNICATION — 115
12	MANAGING CONVERSATIONS	117
13	INDIVIDUAL SAFEGUARDING	123
14	INDIVIDUAL STRUCTURAL PREPARATION	127
15	RESPONDING: STRUCTURAL EXECUTION	135
16	STRUCTURAL SAFEGUARDIN	142

17	COMMUNICATING CLEARLY	144
18	MANAGING UNWANTED OUTCOMES	151
19	COMMUNICATING YOUR OWN NEEDS	155

PART V PREVENTION — **159**

20	A CASE FOR PREVENTION	161
21	RESPONDING: EDUCATION EVOLUTION	165
22	PREVENTING: REGENERATION	170

Index — 175

Acknowledgements

Firstly, I would like to acknowledge unwavering support from my fiancée Daniel Johnson, who fuelled this book with cups of tea and encouragement! Without both, this book would not have happened.

Secondly, Cath Kitchen in her aspirational and inclusive approach of starting with the child and the family, rather than them fitting in with an overall system. Throughout the last few years she has inspired me to do better for the child we support.

Lastly, I would like to acknowledge Dan Owen, who continues to be supportive in developing ideas of how behaviour is always beyond just what it looks like and to approach things with professional curiosity.

Introduction

About me

At the age of 15, I had already planned to go to college and had sought a hairdresser placement to undertake an apprenticeship. My mum had previously followed the same course and left school when she was 14. My father had left the family home when I was 9, but he too had a similar and typical working-class background of leaving school at a young age and becoming a motor mechanic.

When I collected my GCSE grades with a couple of As, a large proportion of Bs (and yes, some Cs in there too – and probably a surprise to my French teacher that I did that well), I went to see the Head of Sixth Form, Mr Bryant, and asked if I could continue. He was a new teacher to the school, and I often cite him as the member of staff who changed my understanding of education and developed my love of learning. Mr Bryant agreed, and I was soon taking A levels in the sixth form.

I can tell you in detail of the teachers I loved and felt valued by. Learning helped to emancipate me from a difficult home life. It set me free when the world felt like it was trapping me. In the years I have worked with children, I have come to realize that not all children find this. For whatever reason, they too may feel trapped and not know a way out of a cycle of deprivation and educational poverty. Those children may need someone to guide them, to help them develop a sense of belonging in their community. This book hopes to give teachers and educators space to reflect on their own practice and their interaction with students to think about how to achieve this.

Despite my late love of learning, I have worked in the British education system since 2001 and lived through the tenure of several Education Secretaries, a series of different governments and their enactment of various policies. I began my career as a part-time learning support assistant (LSA) in a London college. My role was to support children who were at risk of exclusion, those newly arrived in the United Kingdom and those undertaking work-related courses in subjects such as motor mechanics, construction and bricklaying.

As I progressed through my first degree in sociology and criminology, I became more interested in how education could be the way in which children could climb out of poverty and adverse situations. I soon trained to be a teacher, first getting my Certificate in Education before gaining qualified teacher status through the Graduate Teacher Programme. I was the first person in my family to have finished school successfully – my mum finished school at 14 to train to be a hairdresser, and my older brother was permanently excluded from several schools before leaving altogether. School, for me, was the space in which I felt I belonged, and a place where I was nurtured and supported by some excellent teachers. School was where I felt safe and valued, especially in the latter years of my education.

Since gaining my first degree, I worked as a teacher and in several senior leadership roles in a range of settings, both primary and secondary and in traditional mainstream and alternative education settings. The latter include pupil referral units (PRUs) for children with health needs and those excluded from school, additional resource provision for children with speech, language and communication needs and autistic spectrum conditions (ASC), care home education, college settings and psychiatric inpatient services.

During these years I was successful in completing a master's degree in inclusive education and started to really question how we understand children with 'challenging behaviour'. I wondered what we meant by 'challenging' and how this label could combine with poor educational achievement and low self-esteem to produce a toxic cycle of disruptive behaviour in the classroom and, if not exclusion, the self-exclusion of poor attendance and engagement in education. I wondered how my own experience of schooling, one of positive engagement, could be translated to help vulnerable children who were on the outskirts – marginalized and disenfranchised.

As my career has progressed, I have seen children grow up and live to have families themselves. But I have known too many children who have ended their lives, or had their lives ended. I am honest enough to admit that I have cried when I got home because, despite my careful planning, innovative and, as I thought, engaging activities, children still talked over me, argued, shouted and were verbally abusive. I have been spat at (and on) and pushed. I have physically restrained children when I felt I had no choice in order to keep them, and those around them, safe. I have hugged children when they have cried and when they have celebrated a key milestone. I have watched children pick up their exam results and be disappointed, and others who know that it has meant they can go on to take A levels. I have seen children discharged from hospital, only to return when things haven't really changed for them.

Without doubt, working in the education system is frustrating and emotionally tiring. This book shares dilemmas through case studies you may be familiar with as well as things you will encounter in the future, and provides suggestions that may support you in helping those children feel safe, nurtured and engaged.

About the book

My ontological assumption from the outside is driven by the notion that behaviour is socially defined, is constructed by our interactions and relationships, and what we may accept at one time as being ok may feel very different when performed in a different context. I also believe we must have high aspirations and hopes for children with a range of backgrounds – cultural, religious, ethnic and social. While I offer ideas in this handbook, it is just that. It cannot negate structural inequalities in wider society. That is perhaps another book for a future time.

The book is titled *Behaving Together* as I envisage positive behaviour being achieved through collaboration rather than control. The first point of this is asking ourselves *'How can we work together to improve things?'* rather than *'What can I do to make children behave better?'* In influencing rather than controlling behaviour we can look at ways in which our practice develops relational trust and confidence in us as the adults.

From this perspective, I ask questions about how we might:

- comfort
- collaborate
- influence, and
- sustain relationships.

The ambition of this book is not for you to know more as educators, but comes from a place of wanting for you to do better with the information you have. There are a multitude of books focused on the issue of behaviour in the classroom and the wider school system. This book hopes to fill the gap by drawing on best practice about influencing real change for the children and families we work with and for.

Writing a book feels incredibly daunting, and from the outset I wanted to make sure that a range of strategies, ideas and tools were given to senior leaders, teachers and support staff in helping children feel safe, nurtured and engaged in their learning. I know that whatever it means to type words on a page does not match the experience of standing in front of a class of 30 children keen to learn, or that one child who is demonstrating a huge amount of distress and anguish.

While writing this book, I wanted to give equal weight and consideration to the 'quieter voices'. I wanted to make sure that these voices weren't lost and their needs were held as important and central as the children who are more obvious in the classroom space or around the school. The case studies explore how educators may support those quieter children, as well as the more obvious ones, in the classroom.

In the education system, children's behaviour is becoming increasingly complex, costly and disruptive. Traditionally, teachers and other education professionals have opted to control behaviour with restrictions, punishment and isolation. *Behaving Together* is designed as a practical and informative guide to help teachers support behaviour through insight, understanding and influence. This approach aims to improve not only the behaviour and attainment of children and young people, but also their mental well-being, family relationships and foundations for the future.

The need for a new approach

Freya and Frankie are young children living with their mum, Farhana. Farhana left their abusive father when Frankie was young. She spends much of her time supporting Freya, her 12-year-old with kidney failure, and worries terribly about the impact this has on her younger son, Frankie.

Farhana wishes that parenting came with a handbook. She wishes she knew how to support Frankie. She wishes she knew how to help teachers understand the child she sees. And she wishes she had more time or fewer demands so that Frankie wasn't frequently having to take second priority to his sister. Farhana fears that Freya may never receive a kidney transplant, but also fears that her life will never be 'normal' even if she does.

Frankie's teacher is called Merva and she worries about the impact Frankie's disruptive behaviour has on the rest of her class. She sees that Frankie is 'troubled' but is totally lost as to how she can help him. She has tried talking to Frankie nicely; she has tried offering Frankie rewards and incentives; she has given Frankie detentions and punished him with isolation and restricted privileges. Merva suspects Frankie will end up in a pupil referral unit, and has read newspaper headlines of the 'PRU to prison pipeline'. She wants to do the best for Frankie but doesn't know how to support him without neglecting the other 26 pupils in her classroom.

Frankie wishes someone could understand the things that happen in his head. He wishes someone could help him find words rather than actions to express his anger, frustration and fear. He wants to go to school and work hard like some of his friends do, but finds it so hard just to organize his thinking and listen to what his teacher is saying. Frankie hopes his sister knows that he loves her and that one day he will be able to support his mum rather than fight for her attention.

Freya feels like a burden. She fights so hard to stay alive but also wonders when she will ever be able to live a normal life. Freya would love to be a teacher and help all the children that normal teachers forget. Her teacher does email her work, but Freya doesn't feel like she belongs at school. Her friends have forgotten about her and she feels really lonely a lot of the time – but rather than telling anyone, she finds it easier to just stay out of the way and try to escape her thoughts by playing computer games.

When we think about the story of Freya and Frankie, it is easier to realize why parents, teachers and pupils desperately need us – the experts, the policy-makers and the influencers – to change the way we understand and respond to the behaviour of children and young people. The world, the concept of childhood and the requirements of the education system have changed dramatically, and the behaviours of children have changed as a result. Today, it is far too simplistic to assume that 'naughty' children are choosing to be 'naughty' and should be punished. Today, our understanding of mental health is far too sophisticated to write off angry children as horrible kids, and our commitment, as teachers, to provide every child in the UK with an education means it is essential for us not to give up on the children who simply don't fit it.

This handbook is designed to address just one piece of the puzzle. We cannot solve everything in one text, and one person cannot know enough to solve these issues alone. At the end of this book, there are many peers and colleagues I recommend for support with the other parts of the puzzle – but for now,

I focus on providing you with tools and information to better identify, understand and respond to challenging, complex and disruptive behaviours.

2017/18 Permanent exclusion data (DfE, 2019)

- Primary schools: 3 pupils per 10,000 excluded
- Secondary schools: 20 pupils per 10,000 excluded
- Special schools: 7 pupils per 10,000 excluded

2,686 permanent exclusions were for 'persistent disruptive behaviour'
2,686 permanent excludes were for 'other'
1,037 permanent excludes were for 'physical assault against a pupil'

References

Department for Education (2019) *Permanent and Fixed Period Exclusions in England 2017 to 2018.* Available at: https://www.gov.uk/government/statistics/permanent-and-fixed-period-exclusions-in-england-2017-to-2018 (accessed 27 July 2020).

Part I

Identifying

1 What is behaviour?

Most simplistically, our behaviour is a response to our environment. That response can be voluntary or involuntary, conscious or subconscious and overt or covert, or variations in between. The prevailing explanation and understanding of behaviour is that our external behaviours are a choice and a reflection of our values, principles and personalities.

In today's society, our behaviour often determines our opportunities, our rights and, ultimately, our freedom. Yet definitions, perceptions and understanding of behaviour continue to be unclear and conflicting. Some educational practitioners advocate focusing on the culture of a school, others on the individual child to change their behaviour, and some on the teacher's expertise and lesson delivery. Others may focus on specific system issues relating to poverty, deprivation and access to opportunities.

Behaviour is significantly more complex than any of these factors taken in isolation. Instead behaviour can be shaped and understood in the context of a nuanced understanding of wider society, psychological factors, neuroscience, interactions and sensory factors. Identifying what we see as 'good' or 'bad' behaviour may feel simple, but the reality is that there are huge complexities in being able to describe behaviour. As a teacher, you will most frequently see this in the context of behaviour reports where a child is described as behaving 'inappropriately' or 'disruptively'. What is described as inappropriate or disruptive by one teacher may be seen as entirely acceptable by another. Our own contexts, language and the culture of a school plays a large part in how we interpret what we see. Regardless, these phrases are value-laden, subjectively described, and do little to tell us what occurred, what the precursor to the event was, and what can be done to prevent future issues. Today, in the education system, our behaviours influence the ways we are able to receive and interact with our learning. Our schools are judged on the way we, as teachers, are able to understand, respond to and regulate behaviour. As such, this book is designed to be a handbook, a knowledge base and an interactive resource for when behaviour is at its most complex. It aims to help you do the best by yourself, your school and your pupils.

Behaviour in education

To truly understand behaviour in education, we must understand the variety of factors that are likely to impact the behaviour of our pupils while they are at school. As a way of trying to understand the complexities of pupil behaviour, we must hold on to our core belief that behaviour is a reaction to our environment.

I explore the school environment below, and begin to consider the factors that may contribute to the behaviour of pupils in our classrooms.

External environmental factors

Pupil relationships: Children who are being bullied, victimized or otherwise alienated in school may have lower attendance, attempt to avoid attending school, be distracted in class and avoid group activities. Children with poor pupil relationships in school may develop strategies to avoid contact with others and feel as if they are outsiders to the school community.

Teacher rapport: Teacher relationships are important, and not every child will be able to develop a good relationship with their teacher (which doesn't necessarily have a bearing on the teacher). Children struggling with their teachers may respond by refusing to work in class for specific teachers and even truanting from specific classes. In class, this may mean they do not listen for specific teacher instruction, distract themselves and others, and miss vital components of lesson delivery.

Stimulation: The sensory profile of every child is different; a simple example would be that some work better with background noises (i.e. headphones, busy spaces, etc.) while others need silence in order to concentrate. While it is well recognized that adults prefer certain working environments, this is rarely applied to children. The outcomes of being unable to express and enjoy these preferences may include sensory seeking behaviours (tapping, fidgeting, making a noise), finding it hard to concentrate on set tasks or avoiding the classroom altogether by running away from it.

Internal environmental factors

Self-belief: This refers to the way we value our own ability. For children with a lack of self-belief we may see a lack of engagement, an inability to concentrate, lack of effort in school and homework. We may find that these children find it harder to grasp new ideas or concepts and are less likely to take risks in their learning. Indicators that we use to determine ability (such as streaming classes, testing) can then reflect the results of their lack of self-belief, and become a self-fulfilling prophecy.

Self-perception: We assume that ambition is linked directly to attainment, but there are many pupils who will have huge ambition that is limited or masked by poor self-perception.

Self-worth: If a child doesn't believe they are 'worthy' they are likely to be defensive, angry and disengaged. At school, self-worth can be linked to a child's ability, the praise they receive from teachers, and so on. We may see this as children who do not want to put themselves forward in relation to answering questions or sharing ideas. These may also be children who behave in ways that aim to distract teachers from the fact that they do not understand the work.

These factors, together, give us an indication of school-specific behaviours but, of course, in an increasingly inclusive world where children bring their 'whole selves' to school, this may include their behavioural responses to both internal and external factors that exist in their home lives. Again, I divide them into external and internal factors for consideration.

External home factors

Abuse: Experiences of abuse can have a fundamental effect on children's experience of adults and how they interact with others around them. Abuse can affect a child's feelings of self-worth, as well as their relationships with others. Bearing witness to, or being the victim of, abuse in their homes can lead to children displaying a variety of behaviours in the classroom. They are likely to express a need for attention through either positive or negative behaviour. Children may mimic the behaviours they have witnessed or experienced, using abusive language or actions. Younger children are more likely to enact trauma and abuse in their play, compared to older children. These are all likely to affect the way they are able to tolerate independent tasks, work in groups and engage in lessons.

Poverty: Poverty can hamper a child's education in a number of ways and is associated with increased prevalence of both physical and mental health concerns. In a classroom setting, poverty may present itself as an inability to concentrate, withdrawal or exhaustion. In some instances, the injustice children feel about poverty may lead to feelings of anger and disconnection from their environment, with limited means to express this in their school. Additionally, those living in poverty may have limited access to resources – whether that be a laptop, a space to complete work or even breakfast – to make sure they are in the right frame of mind. Children may have fewer opportunities to engage in extracurricular activities, such as visits to museums or galleries, as the cost of travel could be prohibitive. This may lead to disengagement and lack of interest in class as children fail to understand the relevance of what they are learning in class to the outside pressures they experience.

Hunger: While free schools meals in the UK have attempted to bridge the gap between children who live in poverty and their access to resources, the use of food banks has increased in the last few years. It is unsurprising that feelings of hunger can cause irritability, difficulty in concentration, tiredness and complaints of physical symptoms such as headaches or tummy aches.

Discrimination: Despite dialogue around discrimination being a key factor in inequality in education for many years, children who are African-Caribbean, from the traveller community or who have special educational needs are more likely to have poorer outcomes and be excluded from the mainstream schooling system. Wider system issues relating to discrimination have not gone away, despite what may feel like a more tolerant society. Children who suffer from discrimination may present as angry, withdrawn or defensive. Anger may be used to express frustrations of discrimination and present further flashpoints such as arguments between children. If children do not feel part of a community, they may seek a community elsewhere – sometimes ones with nefarious intentions, such as those that wish to exploit their vulnerabilities.

Parental relationships: Attachment styles are used to describe the different ways children develop relationships with a primary caregiver. Most children have secure attachments. They can explore an environment away from their parent and, if that parent leaves, are initially upset, but feel comforted by their return. However, some children, for a range of reasons, may have alternative attachment styles, and this may affect them in the classroom. For example, some children may not trust adults in a way that you would expect, so will appear disinterested. Some may seem 'clingy' and demanding of the teacher's attention. Others may present as frightened, tearful or angry. The way in which a child develops in their formative years has a fundamental impact on their later behaviours.

Sibling relationships: Relationships with siblings are varied and can be influenced by age difference, gender, personalities and so on. Siblings may assess their own progression in education through comparison with a peer (Davies, 2019). Poor relationships between siblings may mean a child feels they are being treated unfairly, and have a further impact on their behaviour. This may be enacted in the classroom by a child being competitive or, conversely, through poor self-esteem and lack of engagement in activities.

Internal home factors

Fear: Children may be living in fear in their home environments. This fear can release stress hormones – often referred to as 'toxic stress' – and the child may be in 'fight or flight' mode. If they continue in this state you are likely to see that they react quickly to things, see threats in things that others see as benign, appear aggressive or violent and avoid making mistakes.

Sadness: Children who are unhappy or otherwise unfulfilled at home can experience an extreme sadness that can be seen in the classroom. It may affect their interaction with their peers and mean they are less motivated to engage in tasks. They may be distracted, find it difficult to focus, exhibit lack of motivation and have difficulties starting or finishing activities.

Trust: It is important that children are able to trust adults with their emotions. Children should trust that their needs will be met and that adults will act in their best interests. In homes where this trust hasn't been established, we can expect children to behave in ways that may be argumentative, disinterested or demonstrate a lack of engagement.

Hope: Whether due to social mobility, discrimination or neglect, children who do not feel hope in their ability to improve their lives or to seek happiness, etc., can become disinterested, disaffected and demonstrate a lack of motivation in the classroom.

References

Davies, K. (2019) 'Sticky' proximities: sibling relationships and education, *The Sociological Review*, 67(1): 210–25. doi:10.1177/0038026118784832

2 Identifying: correlation with known conditions

While formal schooling has been a consistent feature of England's education system, the role of the teacher has changed and developed over time. In recent years, our role as teachers has evolved to include not just being tasked with leading a class and teaching, but developing a range of pastoral skills. We are often asked to understand, support and nurture the children in our classroom and our school communities. At the same time as teachers have been developing a pastoral as well as an academic role, the mental well-being of our pupils has become a critical concern as there is a rise in the mental health needs of children in our communities.

Many of us may have supported our own mental well-being by doing more to understand the symptoms of our mental health conditions. We may use self-help books, the internet and our friends to provide us with additional information to understand how our own underlying needs, experiences and thinking may shape our reactions.

Some of us reading this handbook may have had direct experience of supporting children through the standard channels of treatment, such as referrals to designated safeguarding leads, a school's pastoral team or the children and young people's mental health service (CYPMHS). Much of this work may have involved signposting to other organizations and agencies rather than necessarily understanding the condition a child (or yourself) is later diagnosed with. We may never really know the outcome of our original intervention of passing on information and concerns to someone else. For some more involved in pastoral care and support we may have wondered what more we could have done to support, nurture and perhaps prevent the development of needs of children in our communities.

A challenging part of this is understanding that some of the behaviours we may see in the classroom or beyond may give us the ability to understand or recognize underlying mental health conditions. As teachers, how are we able to look beyond challenging or disruptive behaviours and support our pupils on the often complicated journey to a diagnosis?

Behaviour and mental health are often tangled and intertwined, with a web of thoughts, feelings and action coexisting and contributing to one another. Even mental health conditions coexist, and it can take years for individuals to receive an accurate diagnosis, coupled with trauma and reactions to difficult situations. Ultimately, it is hard to understand something that isn't that well defined and is contested from a range of perspectives.

To try to understand behaviours that may indicate more complex, underlying conditions, I have divided them into the following sections: I explore what is meant by the term 'attachment' in the context of child development, when things don't go as expected or planned in childhood, when children may think atypically, and when children may struggle to understand things that are said in the classroom (speech, language and communication needs).

In this chapter, information will be limited to identifying conditions and issues, rather than understanding or reacting to them. This is designed, primarily, to ensure teachers are more aware of the culture of their classroom, how to adapt and consider the needs of a range of children and the existing conditions that can cause or contribute to what is seen as problematic behaviour when they aren't considered and compensated for effectively.

For ease of use, it begins by looking at attachment as a fundamental building block of understanding children, before moving on to exploring in this order:

- When things don't go as expected in pregnancy and childhood:
  - looked after children
  - foetal alcohol syndrome (FASD)
  - adverse childhood experiences (ACE)
  - reactive attachment disorder (RAD)
  - post-traumatic stress disorder (PTSD).
- When children may think atypically:
  - autistic spectrum conditions
  - pathological demand avoidance.
- When children may have additional difficulties that may make it harder in class or around school:
  - anxiety
  - selective mutism
  - attention deficit hyperactivity disorder
  - obsessive compulsive disorder.

It is important to acknowledge that a number of the specific areas discussed could be incorporated in other sections. For example, FASD may have a fundamental impact on how children may think atypically, as well as having an additional difficulty that may make it harder in the school environment. In organizing the information in this way, the reader is invited to consider overlaps and similarities between potential approaches.

Attachment

What is attachment?

Attachment theory refers to the emotional bond that individuals have with their primary caregiver. The primary caregiver is the main person providing safety and security to the child – often assumed to be the mother (especially in studies about attachment), but there is no reason why it can't be the father or another significant adult. Secure attachments are seen in supporting a child in knowing that the primary caregiver (and other adults) are safe and dependable. These children are more likely to take risks in their learning and be resilient to making mistakes.

Attachment is a cornerstone of psychological understanding of child development, parental relationships and future relationships. The attachment with the primary caregiver is seen as fundamental in developing good mental health. Having healthy (or secure) attachments helps set the groundwork for the ability to respond appropriately to others, to situational stress and to be responsive to events that may occur. Mary Ainsworth developed an experiment known as the 'Strange Situation' which looked at ways in which a child responded when the primary caregiver (in this instance, the mother) left the room. From this experiment, Ainsworth identified four different types of attachment styles:

1 secure
2 insecure (anxious ambivalent)
3 insecure (anxious avoidant)
4 insecure (disorganized attachment).

In secure attachment styles, the child understood the primary caregiver as reliable and dependable. In the Strange Situation, the primary caregiver would leave the room and those children identified as having secure attachment styles would demonstrate upset when their mothers left. However, on their return the child would show happiness and joy. Essentially, the mother would be able to comfort the child on their return. When their mother was in the room, the child was happy to explore the environment around them.

It is considered that attachment styles affect a child's positive internal working model. A positive internal working model refers to a set of expectations and beliefs about the self. This means a set of expectations and beliefs about the self, others and the relationship between the self and others. It is important to note that Ainsworth identified that only 60 per cent of children demonstrated behaviours akin to secure attachment styles, while the remainder fit into one of the insecure attachment styles. Having an attachment style which is seen as 'insecure' does not mean that the attachment style is disordered, though.

Insecure avoidant attachment styles were noticed in the Strange Situation experiment. Children with secure attachment styles were keen to explore the room while their primary caregivers were present and showed upset when the caregiver left, but comfort on their return. Other children demonstrated different responses to the primary caregiver leaving and returning. Though there were similarities with the exploration of the room, if the primary caregiver left the room the child would not necessarily demonstrate upset like the children seen as having secure attachment styles. Additionally, when the primary caregiver returned the child would continue their interactions without necessarily responding to their return. Ainsworth notes that in the family environment in these homes the parent would have little emotional availability, would be perhaps unresponsive to the child and would, in some instances, even show rejection to interaction. This meant that if the child demonstrated frustration or anger, the primary caregiver would not necessarily reassure them. While these children may initially express more anger and frustration compared to those with secure attachment styles, they would learn that their primary caregiver was not emotionally available, especially in instances where the child demonstrated anger. Thus, the child learns to be less expressive with their emotional state.

In insecure ambivalent attachment styles, children in the Strange Situation remained alert to the whereabouts of their primary caregivers even while playing and were upset if they left the room. When the primary caregiver returned they would immediately return to her and the child would appear clingy. With these children, the behaviour demonstrated when the caregiver returned would oscillate between angry outbursts and then being still. It is noteworthy that Ainsworth recognized that, irrespective of whether the child was demonstrating anger or being unresponsive, they were not soothed by the presence of their caregiver. This was irrespective of their primary caregiver appearing emotionally supportive. Ainsworth noted that, in these instances, the primary caregiver was inconsistent in their availability and could be described as preoccupied and not in tune with their child's emotional state. In turn, their child would appear anxious and clingy. Ainsworth postulated that the child would see the primary caregiver as physically available, but unable to comfort them. So, in order to get a response from their caregiver, they would overreact.

A later addition to attachment theory was the recognition of disorganized attachment styles. Over the years, the Strange Situation experiment was repeated. It was noticed that some children responded differently in comparison to the attachment styles identified in previous Strange Situation experiments. In these latter children, when their primary caregiver returned, the child would approach them but then stop and instead move towards a corner of the room. In reviewing this behaviour, it was theorized that the relationship behind this attachment was dysfunctional in nature.

While the primary caregiver is meant to soothe, the child instead has recognized adults as a potential source of risk and danger. The child isn't able to resolve this tension between the primary caregiver – meant to be safe and dependable – and their alternative experiences. The child's behaviour then enacts this conflict and their interactions are seen as disorganized.

When things don't go as expected in childhood

When things don't go as expected in childhood, developmental milestones are missed, delayed or affected. Childhood trauma or insecure attachment types can lead to behaviours that are entrenched in our personalities, our habitual responses to challenges, changes and circumstances.

Some behaviours that might indicate issues in early childhood include:

- inability to maintain healthy, positive relationships
- self-sabotage or self-destructive behaviours

- extreme inconsistency in demeanour
- need for excessive praise or reassurance.

A more complex look at development in early years allows us to explore a range of conditions and the types of behaviours they may contribute to in a classroom environment.

Looked after children

In the UK, the term 'looked after children' refers to children who have been in the care of the local authority for more than 24 hours (NSPCC, 2020). There are myriad reasons why a child may be taken into care, and these are important as they help us understand whether or not a child has further difficulties in the school environment and beyond. For some children, it may be because their parents are unwell and require support while recovering from ill health. Some parents may need respite care if a child has significant and complex physical health needs, and in this case respite is planned. Some children may be unaccompanied asylum seekers under the age of 18. With others, there may be significant concerns about parents harming the child through physical/sexual abuse or neglect.

We can see how the reasons behind a child being looked after by the local authority may provide a deeper understanding of a child's behaviour in the school environment. For some children we may draw upon issues relating to ACE; with others, if we know the mother has a history of alcohol abuse, issues relating to FASD. And for those children unaccompanied from war zones, PTSD may be a specific area of concern.

Foetal alcohol spectrum disorder (FASD)

During pregnancy, alcohol is able to pass from the mother's blood, through the placenta and into the foetus. As the foetus is not yet developed, it is unable to process the alcohol as an adult could. The alcohol can cause damage to foetal cells, including brain cells and the spinal cord. For some women, this can lead to miscarriages; for babies that survive, it can have a fundamental impact on their development and have lifetime consequences. Below, I outline what some of these difficulties may be, and how they may affect a child's behaviour in your class.

Poor balance and motor coordination

You may notice that a child has a poor grip on their pen or pencil, and this will have an effect on the neatness of their writing. Children with poor motor coordination may have difficulties catching and throwing. This in turn can have an effect on a child's self-esteem and relationships with others as they may feel unable to participate in games, or not be chosen for more physical play. They may also struggle to maintain an appropriate social distance from other children, causing further potential conflict.

Poor memory skills

You will probably notice a child with poor memory skills by virtue of them forgetting homework and other resources for the class. This can be a flashpoint for disagreements and arguments with teachers. It can also be a source of personal frustration and may mean that a child withdraws or avoids activities.

Difficulties in concentrating and poor attention

As a teacher, you may find you are repeating yourself or continually asking the child to focus on the activities in the classroom. These children may find it difficult to start and finish activities. In terms of behaviour, you may see this in the context of avoiding tasks, withdrawing, or attempting to distract others to avoid acknowledging their own difficulties.

Specific difficulties in maths or timekeeping

FASD can mean that a child has specific difficulties in maths, timekeeping or social skills. The behaviour associated with this is wide-ranging, but you may see some children 'flare up' and refuse to undertake tasks relating to more complicated maths skills, or avoid those classes all together.

A child may struggle socially

There is evidence that children exposed to alcohol prenatally are more likely to have particular difficulties socially. Children may be more irritable, less responsive to social cues and uncooperative (Kelly et al., 2000).

A child may be smaller than their peers

A child who appears physically smaller than their peers may have more difficulty establishing positive relationships with them. The child may attempt to present themselves as being stronger or bigger than their physical presence suggests. This may be predominant in younger children who have difficulty expressing themselves and their thoughts verbally.

Adverse childhood experiences (ACEs)

Adverse childhood experiences are traumatic events that occur in a child's formative years and affect their development. This includes a child's physical and psychological development. There is growing evidence that being subjected to traumatic events in childhood can have long-term effects well beyond the chronology of the events themselves. These long-term effects may range from unemployment to obesity to poor mental health.

ACEs may include intentional acts from primary caregivers, such as sexual or physical abuse, but also poverty and deprivation, which can lead to neglect.

More recent discussion of the concept of 'institutional ACEs' recognizes that traumatic experiences may occur not only in the family, but in attending school or other institutions that affect a child negatively.

There have been attempts to quantify and predict the effect of ACEs through rudimentary scoring systems – the more ACEs you are exposed to, the greater the risks associated with poor health and economic outcomes. However, I am not going to repeat the arguments here as there is a danger that we start seeing ACEs as a counting exercise and do not recognize the individual nuanced response to risk. Additionally, as a teacher, knowing that a child has an ACE score of 10 compared to 20 does very little to help you understand how to support that child in your classroom and beyond.

Children who have suffered from ACEs may:

- Avoid activities and tasks

   Children who have suffered a number of ACEs may experience poor self-esteem, delayed development and be scared of making mistakes. They may not understand the task set or be fearful of an adult's reason for setting the work. These children may not complete the work or do things like rip it up so as not to show it to others.
- Hide under tables

   Children who have experienced trauma may have heightened responses to worries and anxieties. They have learned that hiding may be the best way to avoid hurt or things that might cause them difficulty. In primary school, you may see these pupils hiding under tables or in the corner of the classroom.
- Throw objects

   Children who have experienced trauma may respond with aggression to try to maintain a distance between themselves and a potential threat. You may find that these children attempt to enforce distance by throwing objects or building barricades.
- Be unable to settle

   Children who find it difficult to settle may fidget and get up out of their seat. They always seem alert to potential threats. This is sometimes called 'hyperarousal'.
- Leave the classroom

   In the same vein as children who may hide under a table, some children who are trying to avoid difficult situations, or what they perceive as threats to themselves, may leave the classroom without permission.
- Challenge authority

   Children may have learned that adults are unsafe, unpredictable and not to be trusted. You may find that some children in your classroom react to these experiences by challenging the authority of support staff, teachers or senior leaders.
- Exhibit heightened arousal or extreme responses to events

   Many of the above behaviours in the classroom and playground are in response to heightened arousal. These children are on the edge and waiting for something to occur. They may have learned that by staying alert they can minimize risk to themselves. You may witness children who respond more quickly or more aggressively to situations in the classroom by shouting, throwing things or showing other obvious demonstration of anger.

Reactive attachment disorder (RAD)

Reactive attachment disorder is the outcome of forming an insecure attachment in early years. Although, primarily, this can be associated with a baby's basic needs not being met (food, comfort, etc.), as we understand more about attachment, we realize that not having our emotional needs met is often equally important and can lead to complications in our mental well-being in later life.

Some behaviours that may indicate RAD include:

- Seeking attention

  Children may have been deprived of successfully being able to get their caregiver's attention. Both negative and positive attention seeking can indicate an insecurity that may stem back to early years. Children may have learned in their initial stages of life that they need to fight for attention, reassurance or support and love. This can often contribute to lying for attention (for example). In class, and especially early years or primary school, you may notice that children find it difficult to explore play resources independently and will need more teacher input to start and finish activities.

- Inconsistent relationships

  If a child has inconsistent care and variations in having their needs met, they too may find it difficult to trust or show others their vulnerabilities. You may find that these children have difficulty in maintaining relationships, whether with adults or peers. One day they may seem to have a positive relationship with an adult and trust them; another day they may seem distant and unresponsive.

- Withdrawal

  You may find that children in your class withdraw from social activities or engagement with their peers. This may be because the fear of rejection is so strong that they struggle to trust others around them. In order to self-protect, withdrawal from the class (not responding to questions, avoiding groupwork, wanting to be on their own) may be a safer option than being vulnerable and seeing their trust exploited. You may find that children leave the classroom, or escalate their behaviour so that they are asked to leave, to avoid engagement with others.

- Challenging expressions of emotions

  Children may experience extreme emotions, not be able to explain how they feel, and exhibit a limited array of emotions and emotional intelligence. This may have a fundamental impact on a range of areas in school, such as difficulty working in groups, responding negatively to failure (i.e. ripping up work or not even starting work) or being aggressive to other children. If a child has a heightened arousal level to threat, they may respond as if threatened, even when the reality is they may not be. You may find they have frequent arguments in the playground with other children as they struggle with social interaction. You might notice that a child appears clingy with specific adults or another child. This can, in turn, be difficult for the individual who is subject to the clinginess. Conversely, some children may be quick to make friendships and just as quick to fall out, causing disruption to the classroom dynamic and associated difficulties with arguments, anger and frustration. Younger children may respond by throwing things or running away from other children.

Post-traumatic stress disorder (PTSD)

The term post-traumatic stress disorder was first recognized by American psychiatrists in the third edition of the *Diagnostic and Statistical Manual of Mental Disorders* in the 1980s. While commonly associated with veterans returning from war, PTSD can result from other traumatic events.

Post-traumatic stress disorder is the reliving of traumatic experiences through nightmares, flashbacks, and so on. What is understood as trauma can vary, depending on the individual. Some key traumatic events may be: car accidents, physical or sexual assault, prolonged bullying or serious illness. It is important to note that not all children who experience trauma will go on to develop PTSD. It is also more likely in instances of interpersonal trauma (i.e. rape compared to a natural disaster).

What might I observe?

- Tearfulness

  Children may appear tearful without an obvious reason and it may be difficult to console them. This may come out of the blue and not really seem connected to events you are aware of. You may notice that some pupils seem constantly 'on edge', emotionally sensitive and on the verge of tears. These may be key indicators of underlying, unresolved trauma and stress.

- Tiredness

  In the classroom, tired children may be unable to sit properly in their chairs, appearing slumped or disinterested. Some children may arrive in class looking dishevelled, rushed or blank. Other signs of exhaustion may be physical symptoms such as eczema or tummy and headaches.

- Seeming distracted

  Children who are distracted may find it difficult to concentrate on what the teacher is saying, and therefore will find it hard to follow tasks. They may avoid starting or finishing activities and you will notice they have not completed what you have asked of them. They may also create distractions with their peers to divert the teacher's attention and try to avoid being brought to task.

- Irritability

  Experiences of being tired, concentrating on other things and being worried about things that have happened in your past may mean you are quick to become angry. You may find that a child with PTSD is quick to anger, holds on to that anger and finds it difficult to resolve.

- Argumentative

  Unsurprisingly, if you are tired, distracted or irritable you are more likely to get into arguments with your peers. You may find that a child who finds it difficult to resolve conflict is more likely to get into arguments with their peers. This could lead to attempts to leave the classroom.

- Re-enactment of the trauma in play

  In early years and primary school you may notice children re-enacting traumatic events through violent or sexual play with toys. Children who have seen anger in their lives may try to make sense of it through their play, or through drawings and mark making.

When children may think atypically

While we may have specific expectations that children will think in a certain way, we know that the unique nature of human beings means that they may not think or behave in ways that we typically expect. However, mainstream schools are often arranged to cater for children who respond in ways that we would not necessarily expect. These can present specific challenges for the classroom teacher and how they may interact with pupils in certain situations.

Autistic spectrum conditions (ASC)

You may have heard autistic spectrum conditions referred to as autistic spectrum disorder, high-functioning autism or Asperger syndrome. After careful consideration, I have used the term autistic spectrum conditions, rather than disorder, and also refer to children as 'autistic' rather than 'having autism'. This is to move further away from the view that autistic children are disordered or can be treated. Instead, the focus on identifying ASC is around supporting children, changing environments and interaction to accommodate autistic children, not trying to change them or how they may view the world.

Children with ASC interact and experience the world in a way that is different from the majority of children. Typically, autistic children may find it difficult to understand what other children are thinking or feeling, may become worried or upset by new experiences or changes and find it hard to communicate with those around them.

ASC is not an illness or disease that can be treated – it is a spectrum, and how people experience it varies. We don't know why some people are autistic. Some parents/carers may describe autistic behaviour that you do not see in the classroom. This is not uncommon, and is often because there are different demands at school and at home. The structures and routines of school can be really helpful for some autistic children; conversely, some children may mask autistic behaviour in school, then let it out at home.

What might I observe?

- Avoiding sensory input

  Autistic children may be particularly sensitive to different sensory stimuli such as touch, noise or sight. You may find that they avoid these experiences by refusing to go into a class, or busier spaces such as canteens. Autistic children may put their hands over their ears or put headphones on to control the noise around them.

- Difficulty with abstract concepts

  Some autistic children may have difficulties understanding abstract concepts or articulating how others experience things. For example, in English, questions such as 'How does the character in *Holes* feel?' may be very difficult for an autistic child to answer. They may refuse to answer or ask for further clarification.

- Following instructions literally

  You may notice that autistic children follow instructions or questions literally. For instance, 'What time do you call this?' in response to lateness may be answered 'Ten past two', rather than the child understanding the implicit meaning of 'You are late'.

- Rigidity in approach

  Autistic children often seem rigid in their interactions and engagement with tasks. Some find that the overwhelming sensory information they have to process makes it feel like things are moving far too fast for them. In the classroom, you may see this as children finding it hard to move from one task to another or to transition from the classroom to other spaces. This may be even more prominent in secondary education where there are higher incidences of movement between classes as children attend classes with specialist teaching staff. Autistic children often have a greater need for predictability and can become anxious when strategies are not in place. You may find they are rigid in applying rules for games and activities and don't understand why others may break these rules. This can be a source of conflict in the playground or during groupwork in the classroom. Additionally, children who struggle with the nuances of social interaction may be left out of games or activities due to a mutual difficulty of interacting with one another. This may bring about frustration, anger or distress as they try to make sense of the world around them.

Pathological demand avoidance (PDA)

The term 'pathological demand avoidance' is seen in the context of ASC, and was coined by Elizabeth Newson in the 1980s. She used PDA to describe behaviours in which a child has an extreme need for control in order to alleviate extreme feelings of anxiety. Their responses are often seen as explosive, out of context and out of proportion to what is being asked of them. PDA is a relatively new psychiatric term, not formally recognized in the international arena. It is sometimes referred to as 'extreme demand avoidance disorder'. There is disagreement over whether PDA does sit within ASC or whether it would be better described as a conduct disorder.

You may see the following behaviours in the classroom or playground:

- Short temper/quick to anger
  Children with pathological demand avoidance may struggle to negotiate social rules relating to turn-taking. They can find it difficult to get on with other people, and you may see them shouting at others if they do not have their demands met. Children with PDA find it difficult to understand the emotions of other children or adults. They may not have the words to describe their feelings of panic, and instead become violent or aggressive, screaming, shouting or throwing things when asked to do something they do not want to do. Some may jump to the worst possible conclusion of an event and, rather than working through the stages, will skip to the end and act accordingly. You may find that some children with PDA have extended periods of rage which may be aggressive and volatile in the classroom or school community.
- Obsessive behaviours
  In keeping with ASC, children with PDA may have obsessional behaviours. These are more frequently in relation to people rather than objects or hobbies. This can be a source of conflict, as a child with PDA may attempt to control the actions of others and not understand that their behaviour is demanding and overbearing. You may see children who find it very difficult to separate from another member of the class, or who appear fixated on a specific individual in the class during the adolescent sexual development phase.

When children may have additional difficulties that make it harder in class or around school

Children with difficulties relating to emotional health and well-being may face specific challenges in the classroom and beyond. It may be that the things that we have already covered (ACEs, attachment, ASC, etc.) are overlapping contributing factors to additional difficulties. Some of the underlying difficulties outlined below may have a fundamental impact on our interaction and engagement in the classroom.

Anxiety

The term anxiety covers a broad range of behaviours and associated needs. Feelings associated with anxiety are driven by biological responses to threats, or what is perceived as a threat. Anxiety is the feeling of worry – the internal experience of being nervous about something. It is a prediction of what is to come and emotions associated with that. Being anxious is not a disorder in itself; it is a way of making sure you keep out of trouble, minimize risks to yourself and maintain your own physical safety.

Anxiety is driven by physiological responses to threat. If a perceived threat is identified, the body reacts to ensure that the individual is able to run away from danger (flee), tackle the danger (fight) or hide (freeze). When a threat is experienced, in order to mitigate the risk anxiety is the body's biological response.

As a physiological response, you – and the children you work with – may notice certain things in your body. These can be, but are not limited to:

- Anger
  When a child feels anxious they may feel shaky, short of breath, experience a fluttering feeling in their stomach and a sense of rising panic. It is unsurprising that children may respond angrily if they are feeling anxious because of their environment, social demands or worries about engaging in particular tasks. You may find they say things like 'Go away', 'I hate you' or 'I don't want to'. As a response to their anxiety, and to provide additional distance from what they perceive as a threat, they may throw things or hide under tables.
- Avoidance
  Children with anxiety may attempt to protect themselves and avoid the feelings that anxiety can bring. The physical experiences of anxiety may mean children feel breathless, sick or have a quickened heart rate. To avoid these feelings, children may attempt to avoid these experiences, refuse to work, run away or not engage in a task. In the classroom, you may see children who withdraw or avoid tasks by refusing to start or come into class, hide in different spaces, run away from the class (more often in primary schools) or truant in secondary school phases. You may also notice that these are the children who do not attend your class at all, and may not come to school because it is too anxiety provoking.

Selective mutism

Selective mutism is an anxiety disorder characterized by a child's inability to speak in certain social settings. There is likely to be variation in when a child is able to speak (e.g. at home or with specific friends) and where they find it more difficult (e.g. school or shops). Some children with selective mutism may respond using signs, while others may communicate with gestures or eye contact. They may have difficulty talking to certain individuals, or to anyone if they believe they will be overheard. Selective mutism is complex, and in order to develop understanding I have highlighted some features that we may see.

Children with selective mutism may be:

- Withdrawn
  Anxiety can be debilitating, and this is a key feature of selective mutism. It may stop children being involved in class and you may notice that a child

with selective mutism finds it difficult to interact with others. They may avoid groupwork, appear quiet (if they do talk on some occasions) and not engage with those around them. They are the children who appear lost and not part of the typical buzz of a classroom. They may freeze to the spot and look frightened, perhaps even more so if you ask them a question – even a simple 'Are you ok?' – though with adults they trust they may use one-word replies such as 'ok' or 'yes'.

- Disengaged
  Anxiety can mean that children become disengaged in the school community and classroom activities. They may respond by freezing, and therefore seem stiff, robotic or unresponsive. They may also seem to be disengaged or not concentrating, as they may need to ask a question to help them understand a task, but be unable to articulate it or feel confident using their voice or alternative means.

Obsessive compulsive disorder (OCD)

Obsessive compulsive disorder is an anxiety disorder characterized by recurring thoughts (obsessions) and irrational behaviours or rituals (compulsions). The thoughts may be images, feelings or urges. The compulsions may be things that we can observe and see, such as repeating activities, or could be internal rituals relating to thinking that we don't see but which can still have a fundamental impact on a child's engagement in class and beyond.

The compulsions are a way for the individual to attempt to reduce the distress that emanates from the obsession. For example, a child may be afraid of doing something they shouldn't, such as standing up in class when they should be sitting down. So, in order to reduce this fear, they may tap the table. The compulsion (the need to act) may not seem rational to an outsider, or even the individual themselves, but still may feel essential to reduce the risk of the compulsion taking place.

What we may observe

- Distracted
  OCD is not just the external enactment of compulsions; there may be a range of internal thinking relating to compulsive thoughts. For example, a child may be counting in their head, or designing an alternative ending to an intrusive thought. This can mean that they appear uninterested in or distracted from a task, and you may see this as being slower to react to instructions or taking longer to achieve, as they are essentially undertaking more than one activity at the same time.
- Repeating activities
  Some obsessive compulsions may involve repeating the same activity over and over again before the intrusive thought is alleviated. This may lead to lateness to class or in completing a timed activity. It may also be a source of

conflict for peers as it may involve having to touch something that belongs to someone else, or even touching someone directly.
- Refusal/oppositional
Anxiety can make it difficult to attend to specific tasks that may relate to intrusive thoughts. This can mean that children refuse to participate in certain tasks and are argumentative, but unable to explain their internal thought processes. Children may have specific arrangements relating to how their desk or the space around them is set, and if this is interfered with can become angry, upset and tearful.
- Tiredness
Compulsive activities can be tiring, depending on their specific nature and how long they take to complete. This might affect an individual child's sleep. You may notice that a child appears distracted, looks lethargic and has difficulty concentrating on classroom activities.

Attention deficit hyperactivity disorder (ADHD)

Attention deficit hyperactivity disorder is often referred to by its acronym ADHD. ADHD is a neurodevelopmental disorder characterized by inattention, hyperactivity and impulsivity. Symptoms can appear between the ages of 3 and 6 years old, and how ADHD presents can change as a child develops. While hyperactivity may be the most significant factor in younger children, this may lessen as they get older and inattention may become a more significant feature. Diagnosis of ADHD is more frequently made in males compared to females (Ramtekkar et al., 2010). There are concerns that gender bias means that girls are underrepresented in the data (Ramtekkar et al., 2010) and their needs not met.

What we may observe

- Inattention
A key feature of ADHD is inattention. You may find that, in the classroom, a pupil may struggle to sit down and stay in one place. They may appear to be daydreaming or not paying attention. Children may be distracted, and find it hard to stay on task or start and finish an activity. They may also appear disorganized – for instance, forgetting their pencil case or homework. This can lead to arguments and frustration, affecting the teacher–student relationship.
- Impulsivity
Impulsivity can present in different ways. You may find that a student in your class talks over you, or other children. They may find it difficult to not blurt out what they are thinking. This may in turn cause tension and arguments, not just with you as a teacher, but also with their peers. It may be that these students act before they speak, so turning to the first thing that comes to them rather than something that they have given careful focus or has been processed. For example, they may throw something to get someone's

attention without thinking how that may affect the other child. They may get into arguments with other children as they respond without necessarily thinking through the consequences. These children may also break the general norms of a classroom, such as blurting out the answer rather than putting up their hand. Again, this can be a source of conflict and feel like a further disruption to the good order of your class.
- Hyperactivity

  Hyperactivity is a core element of ADHD, even featuring in its name as well as being a diagnostic feature. In the classroom, this may be seen in behaviours such as the child struggling to sit down and stay in one place, which can lead to them not engaging in a task and being in conflict with their teacher. You may come across children who struggle to work in groups because they find it hard to process tasks in a systematic way and are distracted by external stimuli.

References

Kelly, S.J., Day, N. and Streissguth, A.P. (2000) Effects of prenatal alcohol exposure on social behavior in humans and other species, *Neurotoxicology and Teratology*, 22(2): 143–9. doi:10.1016/s0892-0362(99)00073-2

NSPCC (2020) *Looked After Children*. Available at: https://learning.nspcc.org.uk/children-and-families-at-risk/looked-after-children (accessed 23 August 2020).

Ramtekkar, U.P., Reiersen, A.M., Todorov, A.A. and Todd, R.D. (2010) Sex and age differences in attention-deficit/hyperactivity disorder symptoms and diagnoses: implications for DSM-V and ICD-11, *Journal of the Academy of American Child Adolescent Psychiatry*, 49(3): 217–28.

Part II

Understanding

# 3 Understanding

Before we are able to understand others, it is vital for us to understand ourselves. Regardless of our profession, our mental well-being, life experiences or even mental illnesses will influence how we interact with others, and how we understand those interactions. To help understand the behaviour of others, both self-reflection and understanding are important components. This is one of the reasons why clinical supervision is routinely used in medical settings. While this book isn't a self-help guide for your own mental health or even your adult behaviours, it still remains important to hold these in mind when thinking about others. Ultimately, this book focuses on the behaviour of children, while emphasizing the need to consider our own positioning and how this may influence the behaviour of others around us and shape the culture of a school.

In preparing ourselves, we should consider our own body language and communication. If we develop strategies where we appear open, and tolerate the messages that children provide us, we can have a better chance of understanding the messages behind their behaviour. Some things to consider – but difficult to achieve 'in the moment'! – are:

- Neutral expression

  A neutral expression can be particularly difficult to manage if you find there is a child in your class or school community behaving in a way that you find scary, abhorrent, frustrating or disrespectful. A neutral expression is not about communicating that you are tolerating such behaviour; it is being mindful that staying composed may help minimize the duration of such events. It may be easy to frown, squint your eyes in disgust or look away in disdain, but this may not help ameliorate the situation. On the other hand, smiling, laughing or trying to make light of a situation may appear disingenuous. It is important to recognize that you have the best understanding of your students, so in some instances these reactions may be appropriate. However, for students you feel less certain about, or in moments of extreme arousal or anger, a neutral expression may help as there is nothing the child can 'bounce off' and reflect in their own actions. Taking a deep breath, or focusing on something outside of the situation – the noise of the next classroom, birds in the playground – may help to keep you in the present moment.

- Open and non-threatening body language

  Being 5 foot 1 in height, I have the benefit of rarely seeming physically threatening! However, it is still important to recognize your own physicality and make sure you do not appear threatening or confrontational. If you are a taller teacher, you may find that standing over a child makes them anxious – especially primary children, where the height difference is more pronounced. So rather than standing over a child to instruct them, bend down or sit down next to them. Try to approach a child face on rather than from behind. This is especially important in subjects such as information technology, when children may have their backs to the classroom and be facing a computer. Position your arms by your side rather than crossing them in front of you, and avoid pointing gestures as they may make the child feel uncomfortable.

- Calm and reassuring tone of voice

    When a child is shouting it is very hard not to increase the volume of your voice to be heard or to try to make your point clear. However, when you raise your voice, what you are saying often becomes unclear or unintelligible; it also starts a back and forth interaction when each one of you is shouting to be heard. Instead, lower your voice and slow it down. Don't ignore abuse, but recognize it as potentially a response to a perceived threat. Using pre-made scripts can be helpful – for instance, 'Daniel, I can hear you are upset right now. Can you tell me what has happened?' is a way of recognizing the emotion.

- Suitable environment

    A suitable environment can be seen as one where each party feels safe. For some, this is about moving away from other young people or to a quieter space in the classroom. Sometimes, sitting opposite a child and having direct eye contact can feel confrontational. You may have little control over the classroom or school environment, but you can make subtle changes to how the environment is experienced by you and the children in your class. For example, in a situation where a child is in a heightened state of arousal, and it feels safe to do so, try sitting to their side. Or ask them to go for a walk with you around the school grounds so you are standing side by side rather than sitting opposite one another. Having worked in pupil referral units and alternative provision (AP) for many years, I have had the opportunity to drive children and young people to places – for instance, for reintegration meetings at their mainstream school – and have often found that the fleeting eye contact in the rear-view mirror can put them at ease.

Having thought about your body language, tone of voice and where you might position yourself, you can also employ aspects that help to protect yourself mentally. One of my colleagues says, 'You can't be everything to everyone', and that is important to hold on to. You can't be perfect. You won't manage to do everything correctly all the time. Sometimes you will get it wrong. In realizing your own imperfections, you can understand that the outcome may also not be perfect, but at least you will have done your best in a difficult situation.

The XY axis – beyond a label

Figures 3.1 to 3.10 look at different behaviours we may see in the classroom:

- attention seeking
- sadness
- defiance
- apathy
- intolerance
- insecurity
- withdrawal.

Each grid is divided into two components, and presented as quadrats (the XY axes). As we begin to look at the number of factors that can influence the way we behave, the complex and unique nature of individuals' behaviour becomes alarmingly apparent. With so many factors that can influence behaviour in various ways, at so many different times, the way we describe behaviour begins to feel at best inefficient and at worst potentially damaging.

For example, Tommy, the subject of the case study that follows, was described as an 'angry' boy. Describing an individual as angry, even at its most basic level of functionality, is subjective and generalized. When the word is used to describe the unique and nuanced responses to the plethora of factors we looked at in the previous section, we begin to see it is very limited, potentially dangerous and arguably even neglectful.

Attention seeking

As an example, the grid in Figure 3.9 is divided into consistency of attention seeking behaviour and whether or not the attention sought is characterized as positive or negative. You will see that attention seeking can be understood in several different ways:

- positive nature with inconsistent behaviour
- positive nature with consistent behaviour
- challenging nature with inconsistent behaviour
- challenging nature with consistent behaviour.

Rather than just saying 'attention seeking', using the grid in Figure 3.9 we can start to build a better understanding of a child's needs. For example, we might see the child who wishes to seek positive reinforcement consistently (think about the child who offers to help clear up class during breaktime) compared to the child who seeks negative reinforcement (the child that throws their work across the room and refuses to leave the classroom when requested).

The grid also allows us to understand the persistency of the behaviour. Does the child frequently attempt to elicit a response from their teacher, every day perhaps, or is it inconsistent? How we notice this behaviour may have a fundamental impact on how we support that child in developing coping strategies for learning in the classroom.

> Tommy was 5 years old when he was first given a fixed-term exclusion for persistent disruptive behaviour in primary school. Tommy would often run out of class. He was reported to not listen to the adults around him, and his mum was often telephoned to say that her son was 'beyond the control of the school'. Tommy had further fixed-term exclusions from school for spitting at staff – Tommy said he was blowing 'raspberries' because he didn't want to do what the teacher had asked.
>
> After several months of repeatedly being excluded, with Tommy running away from his teachers and not engaging with his learning, he became increasingly aggressive towards staff. Tommy was becoming more and more distressed, and his behaviour then escalated to undressing and threatening to urinate on the window sill. For this, Tommy was permanently excluded. He began to attend the local pupil referral unit (PRU) on a part-time timetable for two hours, three days a week.

This case study gives us a sense of noticing Tommy's behaviour but we do not necessarily understand what is behind his behaviour. Tommy was later diagnosed with two overlapping conditions: pathological demand avoidance (PDA) and autistic spectrum condition (ASC). Both of these are likely to have had significant implications for his external behaviours. Moreover, Tommy and his mum both reported a lack of support from the school. There appeared to be a lack of anticipation of his needs (*what Tommy might require*) and therefore a lack of consideration of appropriate adjustments that could support him. This book does not aim to castigate school personnel and the way they manage really challenging behaviour – Tommy's mother, Emily, is keen to reiterate that the school were trying to support Tommy but did not really understand him or how their interactions with one another affected his engagement in the school community. Instead, as you read through the different chapters, this book aims to give you additional resources and tools to help children like Tommy get the support they need before they reach the stage of exclusion. Learning to teach and what it means to be a teacher cannot be covered just within initial teacher training: it is an ongoing process where mistakes are bound to be made. In this book, I reflect on and am open to my own mistakes because we should all be in a position to learn and develop our practice.

Phoenix Frameworks

In helping children like Tommy, and the other children whose stories are told in this handbook, we have created 'Phoenix Frameworks'. They are based on XY axis charts to start a discussion around the complexities of behaviour and children's needs. Knowing that Tommy has a diagnosis of PDA and ASC may point us in the right direction, but another child with the same diagnosis may present very differently. There is no one solution that fits all, but the frameworks are designed to provide objective language and measurable indicators of a child's behaviour. In basic terms, Phoenix Frameworks help us understand how internal and external factors may influence one another to create significant or subtle differences in a child's behaviour over time or in different environments.

We will refer to the use of Phoenix Frameworks throughout this handbook, but they are initially presented here to help you better identify different behaviours.

The framework in Figure 3.1 explores **anger** and provides a more nuanced way of describing the varieties of angry behaviours. Rather than just saying '*Tommy is angry*', we can begin to explain when, how and where Tommy displays angry behaviours.

Figure 3.1 Identifying anger

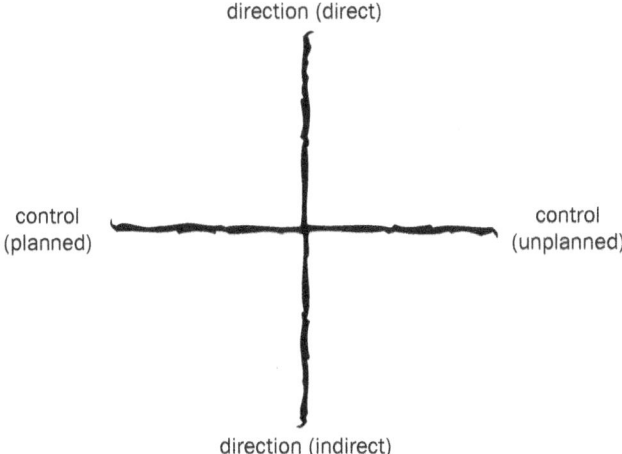

The simple framework allows us to describe anger as:

- ***Direct and planned***: For example, direct and planned anger may describe an attack on a specific pupil, perhaps where the surroundings, peers or weapons needed to be planned or coordinated before the event. Anger of this nature is often controlled and considered. It demonstrates intention and a specific target or focus of a child's anger.
- ***Direct and unplanned***: Direct and unplanned anger may describe a sudden outburst of anger (throwing a chair, punching a pupil, spitting in a teacher's face). Although the action is unplanned, unpredictable and often uncontrollable, it is aimed at a very specific source rather than a general expression of anger.
- ***Indirect and planned***: Indirect and planned anger can describe acts such as rioting or protesting. It might be a planned rebellion in the lunch hall, a lunchtime brawl or acts of vandalism on school grounds.

- ***Indirect and unplanned***: This type of anger relates to an often uncontrolled outburst of rage. Some people refer to this type of anger as a 'red mist', characterized by its generalized, unpredictable and unplanned nature.

Using Phoenix Frameworks for describing behaviour

Phoenix Frameworks have a number of uses, but first we will look at how they can help us better describe behaviours we notice. The frameworks are designed ultimately to enhance the way you observe and describe behaviour, but initially you will probably dip in and out of this resource.

For each framework, there are key thinking points that will help you best position and clarify the behaviour a specific child is presenting. It's important to note that this section is not about understanding the behaviour – here we are focusing on being better at noticing and describing the behaviour that occurs in our classrooms.

Anger

It is important to remember that being angry isn't always associated with violence, and anger can be seen in much more subtle behaviours or changes in a child's tone of voice, their relationship with themselves, the way they regard objects or respond to other pupils. Anger can be seen in interactions with others and also the refusal to interact, and although it can often be a permanent part of a child's personality, you may notice changes in the nature, frequency or severity of a child's anger.

In 1976, Aaron Beck developed a cognitive explanation of depression in which he found that automatically negative thoughts are created by a negative cognitive triad of negative views about the world, about the future and about oneself.

Although this model is used as a framework for the treatment of depression, it can also be utilized in our understanding of anger, questioning if children are angry with the world (I am angry because everything is against me), their future (I am angry because nothing is ever going to go right for me) or themselves (I am angry because I am stupid and ruin everything).

When looking to identify anger, some of the things you may want to ask yourself include:

- Is the anger in response to a specific person or event?
- Can you understand the reason for the child's anger?
- Did the child need to plan or prepare for a specific angry interaction?
- Did the child influence others or manipulate them to also behave in an angry manner?
- Is the child angry with themselves?
- Do you sense that the child is able to control their anger?
- Where do you think the child's anger is directed?

Understanding **37**

The anger framework is designed to help us notice the direction of a child's anger (who or what it is directed at) and the level of control the child has over how and when they demonstrate angry behaviours. Based on your answers to these questions, position your pupil on the XY axis in Figure 3.2.

Figure 3.2 Identifying anger

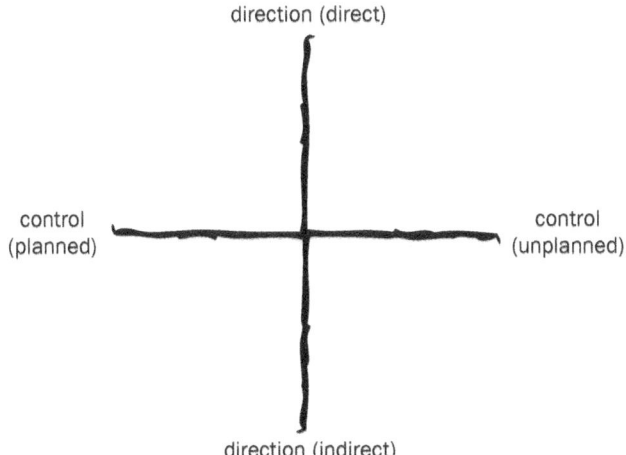

Withdrawal

To be withdrawn can be a physical or mental act of distancing and is often used to isolate and remove yourself from social engagement, interaction and activity. Withdrawn behaviour fundamentally deprives us of the social interaction we need to thrive as human beings, and some experts see it as an act of self-harm and an indication of underlying complex needs and issues. When noticing this behaviour, it is essential to recognize that while many children 'play up', there are others who communicate and express their need through what they don't say and do.

When looking to identify withdrawal, you may want to ask yourself some of the following questions:

- Is the child withdrawn all the time or is it something you notice in particular lessons or environments?
- Do you know if the child is withdrawn in both home and school environments?
- What are the kind of situations in which your pupil isn't withdrawn (small groups, specific subjects, particular times, etc.)?
- What do the situations in which your pupil is withdrawn have in common (is it related to particular subjects, activities, specific pupils, certain times of the day or days of the week)?

- Are you aware of events that happen in the child's home life that may interact with their withdrawn behaviour (interaction with parents or siblings or out of school clubs or activities, etc.)?

The withdrawal framework is designed to help us notice the source of a child's withdrawal and how consistent their withdrawn behaviour is. Based on your answers to these questions, position your pupil on the XY axis in Figure 3.3.

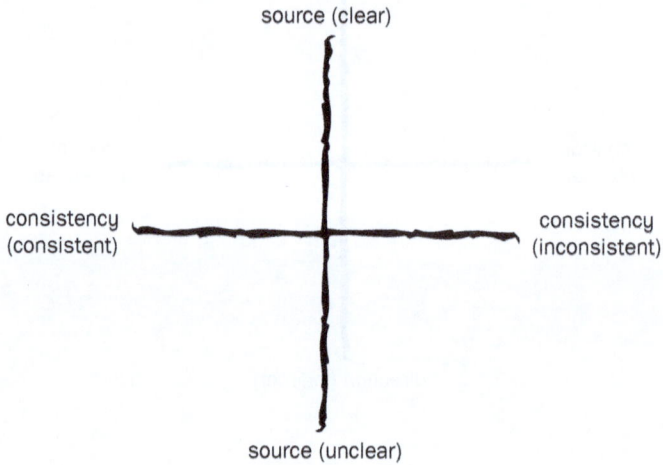

Figure 3.3 Identifying withdrawal

Insecurity

Although many of us relate to feelings of insecurity, for some a lack of confidence can have huge detrimental effects throughout their lives. Despite the general assumption, confidence is not something that we either do or don't have – it is complex, and we are confident in some areas of our lives but not others. Confidence (and in turn insecurity) can be reinforced by external influences, individuals or our own thought processes.

Insecurity and confidence can both be associated with a variety of mental health conditions and self-destructive behaviours. In a classroom, insecurity can contribute to attempts to seek attention, a lack of ambition, focus or ability to concentrate. Lack of confidence may prevent children starting work, finishing their tasks or asking for help. When considering confidence and insecurity, it is useful to recognize that often the loudest children are attempting to elicit a response to combat insecurities and mask their vulnerabilities.

When looking to identify insecurity, some of the things you may want to ask yourself include:

- Do you notice that the child demands either positive or negative attention in your classroom?

Understanding **39**

- Does the child often use self-doubting or self-deprecating language?
- Do you notice that the child tries to avoid group activities or collective tasks?
- Does the child regularly seek reassurance from yourself or others?
- Does the child need a lot of support to start or finish a task?
- Does the child ever seem vulnerable, or are they confident enough to show or share their weaknesses?
- Does the child show fear or resistance to changes or new circumstances?
- Is the child able to maintain consistent and stable relationships with their peers?

The insecurity framework is designed to help us identify what an individual's insecurities are associated with and how the child is able to manage feeling insecure. Based on your answers to these questions, position your pupil on the XY axis in Figure 3.4.

Figure 3.4 Identifying insecurity

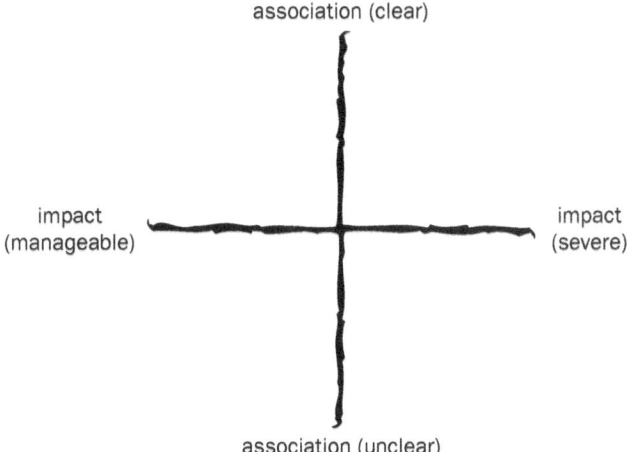

Intolerance

In a school setting, intolerance can look like disobedience, a rejection of authority and a refusal to respect boundaries and rules. Like many behaviours, intolerance appears to be a choice. So when a pupil is unwilling to cooperate it may be difficult to see beyond the labels we associate with challenging children. If a pupil presents us with refusal, it can be hard to see the nuances in their behaviours so that we can describe them more effectively and begin to explore what they might be communicating.

When looking to identify intolerance, you may want to ask yourself some of the questions below:

- Do you notice that the child avoids certain classes, environments or other people?
- Do you notice that the child avoids or ignores certain pupils or teachers?
- Do you notice anger and avoidance rather than structured or effective conflict resolution?
- Do you notice that the child struggles to maintain relationships as you would expect?
- Has the child ever refused to engage in a lesson or a specific activity?
- Does the child often arrive late to lessons, miss detentions or otherwise refuse to accept authority?

The intolerance framework is designed to help us identify how much a child is aware of their intolerant thinking and how much they are able to control how they act on it. Based on your answers to these questions, position your pupil on the XY axis in Figure 3.5.

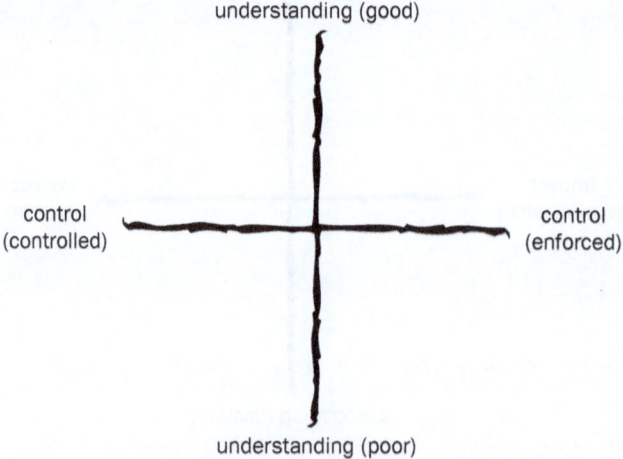

Figure 3.5 Identifying intolerance

Apathy

Apathy is defined as a lack of interest, enthusiasm or concern but is usually characterized by a lack of empathy and appropriate interaction. Apathetic behaviour is a common sign of a variety of mental health problems and cognitive conditions.

Empathy allows us to feel understood and to reciprocate those feelings. In turn, this fuels human connection and reduces stress. We need empathy to understand who and what is good for us and to help us protect ourselves and design a social environment that supports good mental health.

When trying to identify apathy you may want to ask yourself some of the questions below:

- Does the child demonstrate sympathy or compassion towards other children?
- Does the child easily identify and explain their emotions?
- Is the child able to identify emotions through facial expressions or body language?
- Does the child show concern when other pupils are sad, unwell or hurt?
- Does the child seek to interact with others?
- Does the child show interest in topics covered in history, PSHE, English or similar subjects?
- Do you notice that the child seems bored or disinterested in the subject matter?

The apathy framework is designed to help us identify how much empathy a child is able to demonstrate and how easily they can interact effectively with others. Based on your answers to these questions, position your pupil on the XY axis in Figure 3.6.

Figure 3.6 Identifying apathy

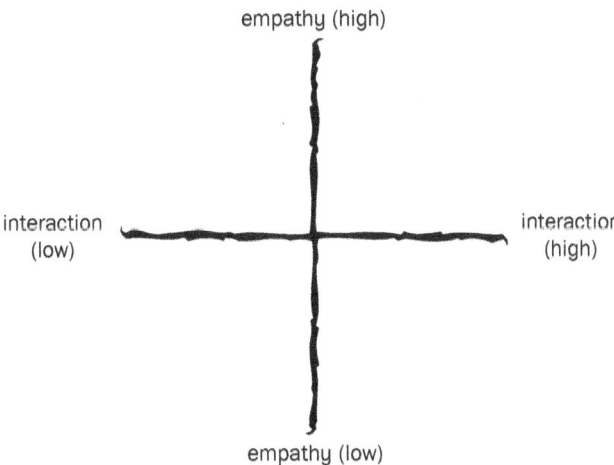

Defiance

Defiance is defined by bold disobedience, which is a key trait of challenging behaviour in the classroom. It is likely to have a significant impact on the other pupils in the class and can take an emotional toll on us as teachers. When a child is defiant, it can feel almost impossible to find any common ground or starting point for improvement and support. This is why it is particularly important to look beyond the label and find the source of the defiance using the framework below.

When trying to identify defiance you may want to ask yourself some of the following questions:

- Do you notice that the child refuses to engage with work?
- Does the child get into arguments or debates rather than engaging with the activity?
- Does the child use disobedience as a means of attention seeking?
- Do other pupils in your class characterize this child by their defiance?
- In which environments is the child most and least defiant?
- Do you observe the child showing defiance with other teachers?
- Is the child defiant with their parents or other influential adults?
- Can the child explain reasons for their defiance?

The defiance framework is designed to help us identify why a child is being defiant, and how strong the link is between their defiance and their identity. For example, some children can show defiance about specific issues from animal testing through to race equality whereas other, arguably more challenging, children are defiant at every interaction with authority. Equally, some children will have periods of defiance that seem out of character, unexpected or otherwise unusual, while some form their identity on their disobedience.

Based on your answers to these questions, position your pupil on the XY axis in Figure 3.7.

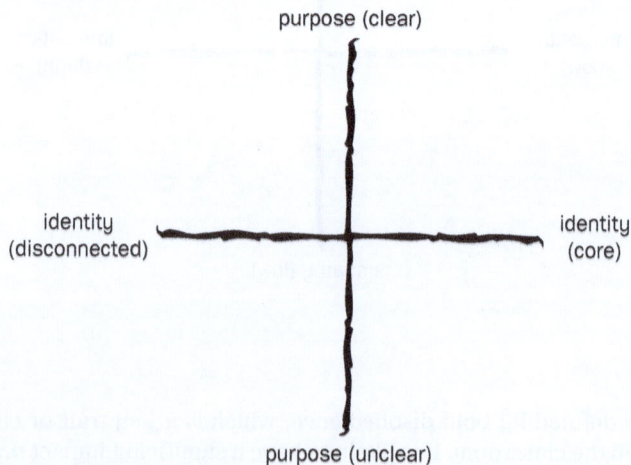

Figure 3.7 Identifying defiance

Sadness

In modern life, sadness seems to be a regular and expected part of our day-to-day lives both in adulthood and childhood. Whether due to peer relationships, the structure of education or influences from home, we will see many children experiencing sadness in our classrooms.

Like any other emotion, sadness has a function. While some argue that sadness has a universal function of letting others know we need help (Ekman, 2020), others see it as an evolutionary response to situational events (Huron, 2018). It is likely that sadness is a way in which we communicate and signal to others. However, it is essential to ensure we refuse to normalize and accept sadness in society, and respond to each child that expresses emotional pain in this way. If children are attempting to communicate with us, we must respond.

It is also important that we are able to distinguish between sadness that is in response to the stressors of everyday life and sadness that is connected to an underlying mental health problem. Think of the difference of being sad because you realize you don't have an ingredient for a meal you were going to make compared to the experience of sadness you may feel after the loss of a loved one, or the experience of sadness in the context of depression. Sadness can be a fleeting moment of disappointment, or it may be ingrained and a struggle to come out of and experience other feelings in any depth.

When trying to identify sadness some of the questions you may want to ask yourself include:

- Does the child seem disinterested or disengaged from tasks?
- Does the child seem to withdraw and not engage in conversations?
- Has the child begun to lose interest in things that they previously seemed to enjoy?
- Has the child been tearful?
- Does the child seem fatigued, lethargic or exhausted?
- Does the child's speech appear to be slower than usual?
- Are you able to identify a source of this sadness in the classroom (arguments with friends, struggling with schoolwork, issues at home, etc.)?
- Are you able to remember other incidents or prolonged periods of sadness for the child?

The sadness framework is designed to help us identify whether sadness a pupil is expressing is in response to something in their lives or could be an indication of an underlying mental health problem that may need medical intervention. The framework looks at a child's understanding of sadness (I know I am sad) and the insight they have around their feelings (I know why I am sad). Based on your answers to these questions, position your pupil on the XY axis in Figure 3.8.

Figure 3.8 Identifying sadness

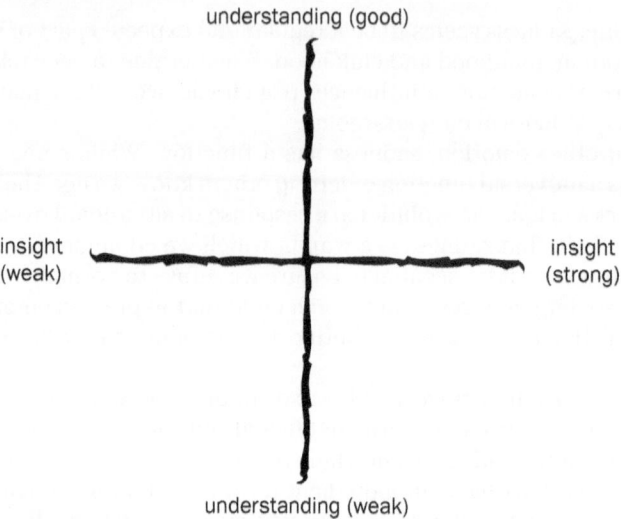

Attention seeking

In every class there are some pupils who demand more attention than the others, and when trying to manage a classroom effectively that can become increasingly problematic. Few attention seeking children will qualify for additional support but the potential they have for disrupting the classroom and interrupting everyone's learning can be incredibly difficult to manage. Understanding the nature of attention seeking is critical, and identifying the cause of a child's attention seeking can provide the insight you need to understand the appropriate adjustments and support mechanisms that can be put in place to support their individual needs.

When trying to identify the nature of attention seeking you may want to ask yourself some of the questions below:

- Does the child seek reward and recognition?
- Does the child behave badly in order to get attention?
- Does the child seek attention exclusively from you or also from other pupils in the class?
- How often does the child need attention?
- Does any amount of attention fulfil the child's need or calm their attention seeking behaviours?
- When is the attention seeking behaviour most prominent?
- Are there any times when the child doesn't seek attention?
- Does the child have a variety of strategies for seeking attention?
- Are you aware of the child fabricating the truth in order to get attention?

- Do you notice that they influence interaction with their peers to ensure they are the centre of attention?

The attention seeking framework is designed to understand both the nature and the persistence of attention seeking behaviour. Consider both positive and negative forms of attention seeking: working hard just to constantly receive praise and recognition is as much attention seeking as constantly shouting out in class. When thinking about the persistence of attention seeking, it's important to consider the amount of attention pupils demand not only from yourself but also from everyone else around them.

Based on your answers to these questions, position your pupil on the XY axis in Figure 3.9.

Figure 3.9 Identifying attention seeking

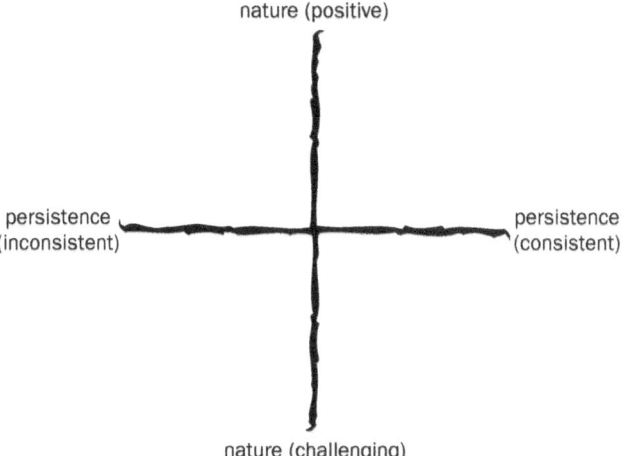

Violence – severity/reinforcement

Serious violence continues to be a critical issue for young people, and understanding the cause depends on all of the factors we explore in the 'understanding behaviour' part of this book. This section looks specifically at violence and explores if and how we can identify violent behaviour in its earliest stages and provide support to prevent the tragic crimes, stabbings and deaths that have increasingly been occurring in the UK and around the world.

When trying to identify the nature and severity of violence you may want to ask yourself some of the following questions:

- Has the child caused physical harm to others?
- Has the child been carrying weapons or other items that were intended to be used as weapons?

- Is the child verbally threatening or violent towards other children?
- Is the child verbally threatening or violent towards you or other members of staff?
- Is the child proud of their violent nature? Do they use this to create status in the school environment?
- Does the child associate themselves with other violent or aggressive children?
- Does the child have any type of criminal record?
- Have the child's parents reported them being violent at home?
- Does the child participate in gang activity outside school?
- Does the child live in an area that is characterized by gangs and crime?
- Is there any family history or association with violence and crime?

The violence framework is designed to identify the severity of violence any child is demonstrating and the ways in which their violent nature is reinforced by society in general and the specific individuals they have around them. Gang culture is often appealing, and therefore reinforced, for children and young people who do not otherwise belong, and who use violence to exert control and seek attention. It is important to note that when identifying violent behaviour, it isn't necessarily about how often children are violent but about the violence they enact and how acceptable they believe this is.

Based on your answers to these questions, position your pupil on the XY axis in Figure 3.10.

Figure 3.10 Identifying violence

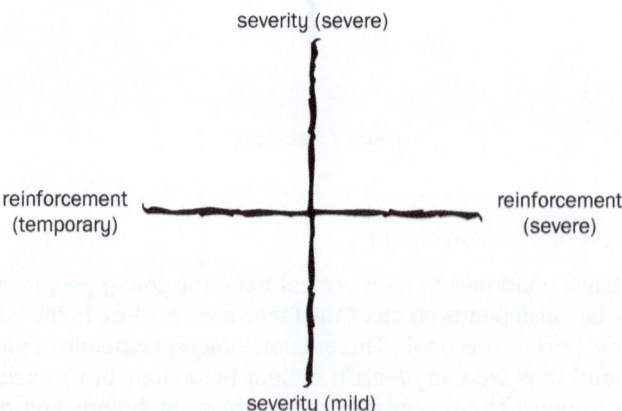

References

Ekman, P. (2020) *Sadness*. Available at: https://www.paulekman.com/universal-emotions/what-is-sadness/ (accessed 24 August 2020).

Huron, D. (2018) On the functions of sadness and grief, in H. Lench (ed.) *The Function of Emotions*. Cham: Springer.

4 Formula of understanding

'Do you need a hug?'

Quite often we may be so busy with the business of schools (teaching) that we may only notice behaviour that disrupts teaching and the learning of others. This handbook reiterates the need to move beyond noticing, and to help those who work with children to look beyond what they see and gain a fuller appreciation of the range of factors that influence behaviour.

In this chapter, I want to start by reflecting on my own challenges in supporting Jessica, who presented with what I initially found to be really difficult behaviour. It was difficult for her, and difficult for myself and the wider staff team. It was the type of behaviour that made me not want to go into work in the morning – not just because I felt threatened, but because I felt stuck in a cycle of what felt like telling off, not being listened to and then a resulting physical intervention. This cycle was not helpful for either me or Jessica. I retell Jessica's story as she taught me as much as I taught her.

> Jessica is 7 years old and attends a specialist resource provision for children with speech and language needs. She is white British and lives with her mum and stepdad. Jessica had a period of fixed-term exclusion from her previous school. When she attended the specialist resource provision she would oscillate from being engaged and focused in lessons to being violent and aggressive. Jessica would scratch, bite and spit. She would scratch and bite herself so that she would bleed. She would pick at scabs and wipe the blood on you. Jessica would attempt to bite you, and on several occasions bit others around her to the extent that one member of the senior leadership team required hospital treatment. Her behaviour felt unsafe, not just for the other children but adults as well. There was a daily routine of punching and kicking members of staff and removal from the classroom. Her behaviour would escalate as the day continued. Despite having an Education, Health and Care Plan and high levels of support, Jessica was given several fixed-term exclusions and there was strong consideration of a permanent exclusion as staff felt they were unable to keep her, themselves or other children safe. We knew that Jessica had needs, but didn't understand how we could respond or provide appropriate support.

Some of you may have been in similar situations; others may be shocked by Jessica's behaviour. Irrespective of our previous experiences, we would all notice Jessica's behaviour, and respond accordingly. We may describe it to others as violent or aggressive, as I did above. In noticing this behaviour, we are forced to respond and react to what we see in front of us.

We might individually respond by being worried about being around Jessica, by talking to her, or by restraining her. We may respond in a wider structural manner by calling meetings with her mum and stepdad, with the senior leadership team or with the local authority. However, in my own interactions with Jessica I didn't understand what was driving her behaviour. Each day I would come into work and wonder whether or not I would be stuck in that cycle of physically restrictive practice. I fundamentally did not understand Jessica's behaviour and was caught up in my immediate response.

After a cycle of really difficult behaviour over a week, I took a lot of time to think and try to understand her behaviour. I visited her mum and stepdad at home; I observed Jessica in other situations; I trawled through her Education, Health and Care Plan; and I began to work out how I could think about Jessica differently. I reflected on her cycle of behaviour and how I might try to change the outcome of a physical restraint. I wondered about Jessica's ability to express what she wanted – while Jessica had expressive language skills, they were limited in lots of ways.

I wanted to be able to understand the interplay between anger, disruption and withdrawal – all the key components of some of the XY axes presented in the previous chapter – albeit without the help of these grids. I wanted to be able to move through the five-stage formula (see Figure 4.1 below), even though this hadn't formalized in my head as yet. The outcome – and let me be clear, there was a long road to getting there! – is detailed in revisiting Jessica and the following interactions.

> Jessica was in the classroom with her teacher. There were only ten other children in the class. She started to shout and run around, but it wasn't clear what she wanted. Usually, at this stage, her behaviour would escalate and staff would possibly be injured. Normally I would ask Jessica to leave the class. Today, instead, I bent down slowly. I wanted Jessica to know that I cared about her and wasn't afraid of her, that I saw her as a lovely 7-year-old girl and really wanted the best for her. On my knees, I used a visual card around my neck which represented a stop card and asked, 'Do you need a hug?' Jessica nodded and said 'yes', then threw her arms around me. Hugging a child in distress felt like a physical intervention that was about showing I cared, rather than a physical intervention which was physically tiring and, often as not, resulted in muscle ache if not bruises (for the staff rather than Jessica).

I had noticed Jessica's unruly behaviour; it is difficult not to in those circumstances. But I had not understood that it was driven by her need for physical

Figure 4.1 The five stages of responding

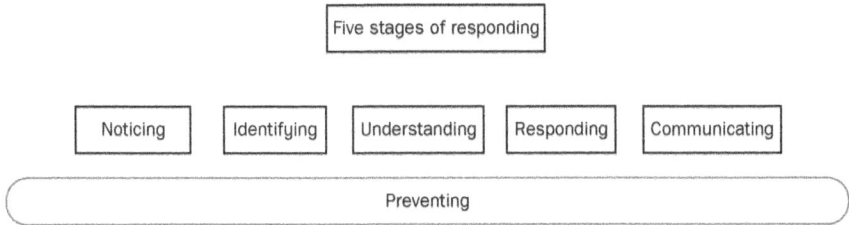

contact, but not knowing how to ask for what she wanted. It is important to note that, while touch may be a powerful therapeutic tool and can be a way of showing positive regard, it may be overwhelming for some children. Adults too may not be comfortable with this approach and feel that it crosses a boundary from professional to personal – especially in secondary settings. Touch is personal and should only be used in the context of a school's policies, when it is conducted for the purposes of the child and not the adult, and with the parents' and child's consent.

For me, the five-stage formula is an essential behavioural management tool – one where we can embrace a deeper understanding of children's needs while using the XY framework to develop a nuanced understanding of those needs. My experience took over 14 years beyond my newly qualified teacher year, and I was – and am – still learning.

The five stages are:

1 **Noticing** behaviours that are presented
2 **Identifying** the need
3 **Understanding** why the need exists
4 **Responding** to the need
5 **Communicating** to wider stakeholders.

Essentially, the five stages underpin the values of moving beyond noticing (that of 'bearing witness') to creating an environment that will help support a child who is demonstrating behaviour which makes it hard for them (and in some instances others) to engage in their learning.

The five-stage formula of understanding aims to support teachers, the pastoral staff team and senior leaders in considering a framework to understand children beyond the context of a crisis, and see it as a strategy for guiding conversations beyond punishment or consequences. The formula should be utilized to gain a greater depth of personalization to a child and be used with the wider XY framework to help shape our thinking and development of plans, with the aim of making a real difference to our responses to children as well as their responses to us. The overall aim is to build a school culture that recognizes children's needs in the wider context of individual psychology, family dynamics, community, deprivation and a whole host of things that affect how we may behave and present at any given time.

Sometimes we can jump to providing a value-laden decision in response to a child's behaviour, rather than moving through the five stages. This may be especially true where we feel uncomfortable with, dislike or are even appalled by the behaviour. The disgust response can replace the professional curiosity that may be helpful to work through the three stages. We may move from **noticing** straight to **responding** and then our overall communication is affected. Critically, we have missed **identifying** and **understanding** and responded with our base instincts to react to a situation that may threaten, scare, frustrate or annoy us. This is understandable – being a teacher does not stop you from responding in an altogether human way! With the judgement comes the potential that we will not be in a position in which we can really identify what the need is and how to understand it. This handbook focuses on using the five stages of understanding to prevent difficult behaviours in class.

The following example is based on a child that I have met, as with all the children I discuss (I reluctantly call them case studies, as I think this reduces children into stereotypes). However, many details are omitted in this case as it was a passing observation when I visited a secondary school. My observation told me that the member of staff skipped several stages, and the discussion moved towards argument rather than effective strategies to prevent an escalation. I will add that as this was an observation, a passing moment, I do not know the whole host of conversations, debates and support this child may have received prior to my observation.

I was sitting in the reception area of a large secondary school in London. My meeting started at 9 a.m., and it was just after. I was told by the receptionist that there had been an issue in the wider school and that the pastoral lead I was meeting would be late. This was not unusual: visiting several schools across the week means that this is a typical feature as schools are busy places. As I sat and waited I noticed a boy come in from the reception area. The foyer was quieter, and I assumed that most of the children were in their classes. He approached reception. The boy was about 15 years old, but it was hard to tell – I would say year 10 judging by his size. He was a black boy and the receptionist seemed to be of Punjabi origin, maybe in her forties.

'Why are you late?' she asked.

'I missed my bus', he replied.

I focused my attention on the boy. He looked dishevelled, his school tie wasn't on yet. He looked tired, and to be honest he didn't look like he was wearing a clean school uniform.

'Get your tie on and get to class!' Her tone of voice was sharp, quick, even angry. 'It is unacceptable to be late. You will need to talk to Mr Griffin at breaktime about your behaviour.'

I was struck by the irony of me sitting there waiting for someone who was late while a child in front of me was being berated for the same crime, and this was likely to shape my own understanding of the situation. Below I have illustrated some key points about this dialogue:

'Why are you late?' she asked. (Noticing, Communicating)

'I missed my bus', (Communicating) he replied. I focused my attention on the boy. He looked dishevelled, his school tie wasn't on yet. (Noticing) He looked tired, (Noticing) and to be honest he didn't look like he was wearing a clean school uniform. (Noticing)

'Get your tie on and get to class!' (Communicating) Her tone of voice was sharp, quick, even angry. 'It is unacceptable to be late. You will need to talk to Mr Griffin at breaktime about your behaviour.' (Responding, Communicating)

Noticing

We have already discussed noticing as a key component and initial stage of understanding behaviour. Noticing – being aware of, and in tune with, what is happening around you – is vital. This needs to include noticing beyond yourself, and noticing how children may respond to the classroom environment, in the playground, to different teachers, to their peers, and how they respond to the school culture that is fostered. For example, do you notice that they find things harder in certain situations? Or if they are late transitioning from one class to another? Do you notice that things seem really difficult for them on a Monday and Friday?

In the observation above, the receptionist is in a key position to notice things others may not. She notices that the boy is late and responds by asking, 'Why are you late?' I notice (I don't know if the receptionist does as well) that:

- He looks tired.
- He is not wearing a clean uniform.

There is a potential jump to responding without going through the other aspects of the five-stage formula.

Identifying

We have looked in detail at ideas around identifying what we notice with ideas presented beyond a label of 'angry', 'frustrated' or 'withdrawn' and looking at specific correlations that we may see in the context of neurodiversity, complex mental health needs and psychological trauma. In this case, there is a lack of identification beyond 'noticing'. There are other clues in his demeanour and presentation that are missed.

- He looks tired.

Some questions that might help us here are: Did you not have a good night's sleep? Why are you late? Is everything ok?

- He is not wearing a clean uniform.

This is more sensitive, and inappropriate for discussion in an open arena. But in order to move towards understanding we need to identify why his uniform is dirty. Is it because his parents/carers just didn't get round to cleaning it? Is it that he is expected to clean it but didn't? Did he simply put on the wrong uniform or brush against something dirty on his way in? Or is this a sign of neglect, and apathy with his appearance?

Understanding

You can see noticing things as clues – a way that you might try to understand things better. As part of this it is important not to be biased or to cling to preconceived ideas shaped by just your own experience.

For example, I worked with a boy from the Hassidic Jewish community who would always wash his hands before eating in a very particular way. A member of staff questioned whether or not this was a compulsion in keeping with OCD. However, in presenting this question to a diverse team who understood some of the cultural practices of Judaism, it was simple to say how this was completely in keeping with typical Jewish practices. Understanding does not have to be complicated or even lead to ongoing concerns, but is simply a way of developing an awareness.

Moving back to the observation of the boy and the receptionist, there seems to be a significant lack of understanding. I think that is partly because we become frustrated with a child doing the same thing over and over again – but the receptionist (or caretaker, or midday supervisor, etc.) is just as key as other members in the school community to understanding some of the behaviours they may be seeing in children, as they are often in a really good position to notice, and if they ask the right questions, identify an issue. If we were to use the five-stage formula to work through to 'communicating' we might begin to develop sympathy and tolerance for what we see as frustrating (the lateness).

In asking a question, 'Why are you late?', there is an initial attempt to understand, but the frustrations revealed in the receptionist's voice do not provide a space for the child to open up in more detail. Now it may have just been that this child is disorganized without any underlying reason, but what happens if we use the five-stage formula and imagine a change in the conversation?

This is where I use my discretion as an author to 'play' with the dialogue to open up the conversation, rather than close it off.

'Oh no! That is a pain, what happened?' (Communicating)

- 'I am so tired, I really tried to get to sleep last night but just couldn't.'
- 'I was at football practice late last night and I really hurt my ankle.'
- 'I've no idea – just really struggled getting out of bed this morning.'
- 'My mum has just had a baby and she came home last night with my new brother.'
- 'I had a massive argument with my dad.'
- 'My mum was arrested last night and I was worried about her.'
- 'My grandmother broke her leg and she was discharged from hospital. We went round to make sure she was ok.'

While we have previously noticed the lateness, until we prompt and ask further questions we may not really understand the background to this. Depending on the answer (and I have explored the different things that I have heard in the past to give a range of contexts), we would then move on to the next stage of how that influences our responses.

Responding

When we look at the stage of responding, we recognize that responding 'like for like' – such as meeting anger with anger – does not necessarily improve a situation. Responding comes from a number of avenues: from us as individuals, and how we might manage in the context of our professional relationships.

Responding also includes what is available for us in the wider context: what is around structurally to support a child, and what we can draw on to help support a child who is presenting with challenging behaviours.

Again, drawing our attention back to the case study I noticed that there was a clear response from the staff member individually and an attempt to draw in others from a wider structural perspective ('talk to Mr Griffin'). There was no sense that there was acceptance of the behaviour, but I do not believe the response was appropriate to the act of lateness as the whole step of understanding had been missed.

Communicating

A key factor of helping a child is in relation to how we communicate plans, ideas and proposed support with those who support the child beyond the school gates. In order to help the child the most we need to make sure we are in a position where we take into account the child's needs in the context of the family, and how we use compassion and kindness as well as practical strategies to help the individual.

5 Cognitive contributors

We run the risk of labelling every aspect of the behaviours we witness, and many cognitive differences fall victim to these assumptions/stereotypes. An interpretation of cognitive differences tends to divide people in their views and become the focus for heated debates around how we should approach children and the way they present.

Cognitive differences are often seen as a way of excusing the behaviour of 'naughty children' or 'bad parents'. There are also concerns that diagnosis and labelling is potentially restrictive and becomes a self-fulfilling prophecy for children. But understanding cognitive contributors to diagnosis can become a potential for reflection and an accurate understanding of a child's presentation in and around class.

Many conditions may be disputed in common parlance. For instance, you may hear bystanders to a parent with ADHD saying, 'They don't need medication, they need discipline', or 'They need to learn to live in the real world'. These debates often lead to a polarization of behaviour 'camps', sometimes referred to as trad-right or left-wing approaches. While the traditional right is encapsulated by approaches such as those offered by Michaela Community School (see Chapter 14), and the left centres on trauma-informed practice, it is often the children who get lost or hurt in the debate.

In recent years, a growing evidence base has helped us understand the cognitive conditions that demonstrate neurological differences in children and young people that are often described as atypical. The term 'adolescent brain' has come to the forefront for those who work with teenagers. Technological advances allow a window into a world that was previously hidden, giving neuroscientists a deeper understanding of what is happening internally and how this links to behaviour. Dr Andrew Curran notes the contradictions between the peak of adolescence in terms of physical fitness and the fact that the rates of death by injury are higher in those aged between 15 and 19 compared to 10–14-year-old children (MHFA, 2014: 113). Curran goes on to detail that scans of growing children show several changes happening during adolescence:

- increase in grey matter
- connections between different parts of the brain increase
- heightened emotional response compared to adults and children
- engagement in different parts of the brain for activities relating to impulse control, emotional content or calculation (MHFA, 2014: 113–14).

It is postulated that these changes may influence aspects relating to responses to emotional stimuli, impulsivity and reduced risk aversion. These considerations should be borne in mind when thinking about strategies to support adolescents. It is likely, because of the particular nature of the development of the adolescent brain, that reinforcement, encouragement and reiteration of boundaries are an important part of a teacher's toolkit. A teacher has a lot to consider, beyond the curriculum and pedagogy, so this is no easy task. So this chapter focuses on helping you to consider and comprehend additional factors that may help you understand a child's behaviour in relation to cognitive contributors. The conditions listed below are not specific mental health difficulties but additional factors that may leave someone vulnerable to difficult behaviours or interactions that may need to be considered.

This chapter moves beyond the stage of 'noticing' and 'behaviour as communication' to understanding some of the drivers behind that behaviour. It focuses on the following contributors to behaviour to help us understand, in order to respond, communicate and ultimately prevent behavioural issues in the classroom:

- autistic spectrum conditions
- attention deficit hyperactivity disorder
- Tourette's syndrome
- speech and language development.

Autistic spectrum conditions

In Chapter 2 I identified some things we may see in the school environment. These were: *avoiding sensory input, difficulty with abstract concepts, following instructions literally* and *rigidity in approach*. We noticed things without building on how we understand them and how they might contribute to the difficult behaviours we encounter.

Though today our ability to identify autism in children and young people is far greater than it once was, our understanding of the neurology of autism remains in its infancy. The interplay between genetics, cognition, psychology and biology in ASC helps ensure that understanding their effects in the behaviours of children is complex and requires a nuanced understanding.

A number of differences have been identified between autistic children and those with typical development. These are not fully understood or explored, but there are suggestions that there are differences in neuroanatomy (the neural structures of the brain) and neurophysiology (how the nervous system functions). For example, there seem to be differences fairly early on in a child's development, with brain differences seen as early as 18 months old. The use of magnetic resonance imaging (MRI) has shown differences in certain parts of the brain. These include an increase in cell density in the amygdala as well as its actual size (Baron-Cohen, 2004: 1) A core function of the amygdala is how we experience emotions. While the amygdala is a relatively small part of our body (the size of two almonds), it plays an important role in memory, decision-making and our emotional responses. All three of these are fundamental to our learning and how we approach learning in the classroom. Another difference between those with typical and atypical development is with the activity in the brain as well as differences in brain volume in specific areas such as the cerebellum (Baron-Cohen, 2004: 1).

Knowing this helps us understand why we may identify some of the behaviours we spoke about in Chapter 2. In a broad sense, this means autistic children and young people:

- process information differently to the way we may expect
- may be overstimulated or understimulated by different environments and sensory input
- may interpret verbal or non-verbal cues differently
- may have additional difficulties relating to mentalization – understanding the emotions of others
- may have different perceptions of threats, risks and danger and respond accordingly.

In terms of what this really means for us as teachers, I have highlighted some key issues in the following paragraphs.

You may notice that some children find the usual classroom environment incredibly distressing and become disruptive in order to communicate this. For example, to them noticeboards, working walls and general classroom displays may feel very 'busy' and be distracting. If you couple this with the general noise of the classroom you can understand that the sensory input may feel uncomfortable and even painful.

Some children will have a differing response to silence and noise. For example, some children may require a gentle noise in the background to help them concentrate; others will be completely distracted by it. In terms of sensory input, some children may have greater difficulty in being able to differentiate between the noises that are important for the classroom – e.g. teacher input – compared to, for instance, the humming of electrics.

You may notice the low academic output of some children, despite what seems to be a good level of understanding and ability. A child may not put their hand up to let you know they don't understand, or they may believe that they do understand but in fact find it hard to process or infer specific information. You may notice, in English lessons, when trying to prompt 'What do you think Isobel may think about this situation?', that a child finds it hard to mentalize and appreciate how Isobel may feel. You may be given answers such as 'I don't know' or even 'Isobel is a character in a book, she doesn't feel anything' as a pragmatic response to a question that requires inference.

Autistic children may struggle to understand subtle social clues, and this is likely to have an impact on how they manage social interactions with others. They may find it difficult to understand others, and other children may find it difficult to explain and understand the behaviour of their autistic peers. Autistic children may have additional struggles in maintaining relationships and friendships, and you may find that they are particularly vulnerable to being isolated or bullied. You may also notice that they find it difficult to share resources or pick up on the social cues required for groupwork. Playtime can also be a struggle: for some autistic children, this may be because they don't understand the social rules; for others, it may be a mechanism to avoid playtime altogether, or because of difficulties with the increase in social input.

You may see children who enjoy a restricted range of activities. They may have a particular enjoyment or fascination with certain topics or themes and it can be difficult to get the child off that topic. For example, I have typically seen an absolute love of buses, cats, trains and transformers. These interests may continue beyond an early age and the young person may still enjoy what is perceived as non-age-appropriate activity. Autistic children may be reluctant to engage in topics that do not fit within their narrow field of interest. Some are less interested in play, preferring the company of adults and activities typically associated with older people – such as birdwatching or trainspotting.

You may notice that children are unable to tolerate the sensory input change from one space to another, and find it difficult to manage that transition. This may relate to some of the difficulties mentioned above to do with sensory processing and memory skills, as well as additional demands in terms of social engagement.

As teachers, when recognizing behaviour, it is vital that we take a moment to understand what any specific situation could mean to an autistic child. For example, asking an autistic child to work in a silent classroom may be similar to someone asking you to teach your class in the middle of a nightclub. You may notice a refusal, but when we consider the cognitive contributors we can really begin to understand and ultimately respond effectively. I have worked with children who have had extreme reactions to engaging in play, or because there is a fly in the classroom. Their responses may be as extreme as those of people in real and immediate danger; you may see all the difficult behaviours that we noticed in the previous chapter.

Attention deficit hyperactivity disorder

In Chapter 2 I gave an overview of attention deficit hyperactivity disorder and we looked at what we may notice in relation to *inattention* and *hyperactivity* in the classroom. I now want to go into more depth and look at the driving factors behind ADHD, and how we understand it in the school setting.

Attention deficit hyperactivity disorder has been much contested and assumptions are rife in terms of how it should be managed (rather than necessarily understood). There are a whole host of judgements on how a parent should manage a child with ADHD. Their parenting skills are often judged as permissive and therefore responsible for their child's hyperactive behaviour. Qian et al. (2019) identify a growing evidence base pointing to brain-network dysfunction in individuals with ADHD. In a similar vein to ASC, there is still much to learn about the reasons for and development of ADHD, and while technological advances mean we are beginning to develop a deeper understanding, many questions remain unanswered. However, there is information suggesting that those with ADHD are affected significantly in the prefrontal lobe of their brain (Gracia-Tabuenca et al., 2020).

The prefrontal lobe plays a specific role in controlling cognitive skills, including problem-solving, our memories and judgement. If these are impaired in some way it will have a significant impact on our executive functioning. This means that children and young people with ADHD may:

- react impulsively to events
- find it difficult to organize their thinking due to issues relating to processing information
- be intolerant of the behaviour of others and react quickly without thinking about the consequences
- not take more typical steps in problem-solving.

In considering what this means for us as teachers and educational practitioners, I now highlight how this may impact on the classroom and the school community.

Children with ADHD may find it really difficult to process verbal direction, especially beyond two steps. For example, if you were to say 'Get out your book, turn to page 94, look at the information on that page, then talk with your partner about how climate change has affected Britain in the last ten years', there are several steps for a child to consider. This can be problematic for children with ADHD in deciding what to do next. Due to poor prefrontal lobe functioning, they may get muddled and jump to the last direction in the sentence – talk with your partner about climate change – but not have processed the initial steps of getting out the book, turning to a certain page and reading the information first. Similar behaviour may also be evident when a child engages in written tasks. Rather than planning their work, they may write down their thoughts without organizing them into a logical piece of work where you are able to follow their trail of thinking.

Impulsivity is, broadly speaking, responding without thinking, and we can see that this is likely to have a significant impact on a child's behaviour. It may mean that children with ADHD are more likely to respond quickly to something that has happened, such as swearing at a teacher or walking out of a class without considering the consequences. In studies relating to deferred gratification and rewards, those with ADHD are more likely to opt for immediate gratification, even if the rewards are smaller. In understanding this, we can look at the ways we develop our praise and reward systems later on (Winstanley et al., 2006) – see Part III, Responding.

Tourette's syndrome

Tourette's syndrome is a complex neurological disorder characterized by motor and vocal tics that have lasted for over six months. It is distinguished from other tic disorders by a premonitory urge – the feeling of needing to tic – before the tic occurs. This is often likened to the feeling of needing to sneeze before it happens. Having a diagnosis of Tourette's syndrome myself, I have drawn on my own experiences to help you understand how it may drive behaviours in the classroom, or those reported from home. Tics change and wax and wane. This means that a tic you may have experienced one day may not materialize on another. Sometimes I find I have frequently occurring tics over several months which disappear for a short while, and then reappear without any explanation. It is important to note that Tourette's syndrome has a number of comorbidities – that is, other things that are likely to occur in conjunction with it – including ADHD and OCD.

Motor tics

Motor tics are movements that may include facial grimaces, chest hitting, jumping, twirling, jerking, touching things and eye blinking. We may notice these, not understanding them, and place them in the context of persistent disruptive behaviour, annoying others or just being irritating.

Vocal tics

Vocal tics can include a range of things such as squeaking, coughing, shouting, saying different phrases, repeating the phrases of others, and the kind that presents the most significant issue for teachers – coprolalia – which is using inappropriate language. Vocal tics can be really distressing for the individual, as well as those around them. They may be phrases that relate to the context of a situation, such as being around children and saying 'I am a paedophile', or the knowledge that you mustn't swear because you are in a serious situation, but then overfocusing on this and blurting it out. You are likely to notice vocal tics in the classroom; some find them easy to ignore, but others find them troubling and problematic.

Suppression

Sometimes people with Tourette's syndrome suppress their tics, and try to avoid doing them in places where they may feel uncomfortable. This is not always possible, and it may not even be a conscious decision, but additional challenges arise when a child has to 'let the tics out' as they may come in a flurry.

In terms of what this means for behaviour in the classroom and beyond, we may see that the child avoids certain things to avoid the intensity of needing to tic but wanting the privacy. For example, you may find that a child doesn't engage in groups beyond the class because that is the 'golden time' in which they need to tic. Or you may see a child that has been subdued and quiet in the class, but as they leave the school or go into the playground there may be a flurry of tics (vocal and motor) as they have the scope to feel free and safe in ticcing.

You may also find that some children with Tourette's ask for frequent toilet breaks, as the toilet is a space in which they can tic in private and not feel they are being watched by others. Other children may frequently tap, fidget or exhibit motor tics that you may not realize are motor tics without the knowledge of a diagnosis. And prior to ticcing, you may see that a child is distracted from their work due to the mental effort that is required to not tic. If these behaviours are understood in the context of Tourette's it may help you make reasonable adjustments to support the child and help them feel comfortable in the classroom.

Another aspect of Tourette's, which is not necessarily discussed, is the feeling of being 'different' and 'abnormal'. Making noises, or performing actions that other people don't, can make children want to isolate from others. Coprolalia, in particular, can affect a child's self-esteem, and other parents/carers and teaching staff may avoid them, or ask their children to avoid them because they do not understand the drivers behind the behaviour.

Speech and language development

Speech and language needs are integral to the classroom and school community. Both how we understand what is being said to us (our *receptive* language), and how we are able to make our meaning clear (*expressive* language), have a fundamental impact on our ability to understand the rules and routines of a classroom. Moreover, having developed expressive and receptive language skills can make the difference between being able to express our internal worlds, or finding it frustrating to make ourselves understood and, instead, using alternative means – e.g. pushing someone away rather than asking them to move.

Our development of expressive language happens in the formative years. It begins with cooing and crying, then being able to gesture (pointing or perhaps going towards something), and then the development of words, which are often nouns (mum, dad, apple, dog), simple verbs (eat, play) and prepositions (out), and attempting to control the environment (no, yes). Language development milestones (what you can expect a typical child to be able to do) suggest that by the age of 3, children will be able to use up to 300 words (NELFT, 2009).

A child who has difficulties with receptive language finds it hard to interpret the meaning of others. In receptive language disorder there appear to be difficulties with the language-processing parts of the brain. It is a complicated task to speak words, and the frontal and temporal regions control what you want to say while the motor cortex located in the frontal lobe is what signals the act of talking. If younger children sustain a brain injury (due to an accident, stroke or perhaps epilepsy) which injures the left side of the brain, there is an increased chance that language development will be controlled from the right side. When a child has specific difficulties with receptive language it is thought that these occur because of specific issues in the areas of the brain which process language.

In studies of young offenders, it is estimated that 60 per cent of children in the youth justice system have speech and language difficulties (Bryan, 2004).

This has huge implications. In considering this link between language and social exclusion, the charity I Can finds difficulties with language and communication skills a fundamental issue in how children interact, enjoy being with others and engage in the classroom (Cross, 2007).

What this means in the wider sense is that children and young people with speech and language disorders:

- are likely to process information differently to ways we may expect
- are likely to express themselves, but find it difficult to make their meaning clear
- may interpret verbal clues differently
- may have additional difficulties in how they interact with others
- are likely to have difficulty with turn-taking in conversations.

You may notice that children with speech and language difficulties also have difficulties in their relationships with others. They may be more open to being bullied, impressionable to suggestions because they don't know the outcomes, and find it difficult making themselves understood, and so take, rather than ask. This may not be driven by the impulsivity we touched upon above in discussing ADHD, but by being unable to clearly articulate what they want. While we may notice similar behaviour, the cognitive contributors are different, so how we might respond needs to be different.

Children with speech and language difficulties are likely to find it hard to understand the instructions of others. They may disregard an instruction or find it hard to discriminate between the different steps. For instance, 'Alex, can you stop what you are doing and not keep walking outside', may mean they focus on walking outside, rather than what you have asked.

It may also be that children with speech and language difficulties find it hard to follow the routines of a school environment, which may be very different to those at home. Knowing the order of things can become a challenging task and it may become difficult to organize. This may look like a child being in the wrong place or doing the wrong thing, but actually be a reflection of their difficulties in sequencing events. Children therefore may find transitions particularly hard and find it hard to say how they feel. Rather than telling the teacher that they aren't sure what to do next, they may avoid the transition altogether or try to follow what someone else has done, irrespective of whether or not the child they are following is doing the right thing.

Finally, and unsurprisingly, you may find children who have difficulty making themselves understood by others – whether children or adults – around them. This will have an effect on their ability to join in play, and you may find they avoid playtime altogether rather than engage in the demands of social interaction that can feel confusing and overwhelming. They may also be become withdrawn, as the demands of processing information and expressing themselves may be very difficult. Or they may find things like turn-taking hard (conversation is a complex endeavour) and blurt out what they have to say, or perhaps worse stay quiet altogether. This can have a fundamental impact on an individual's self-esteem as they do not have the positive reinforcement of engaging socially. You may find that these children are quieter in the classroom and become lost in the everyday of teaching practice. How we support quieter students is just as important as supporting those who may be more noticeable in the classroom.

References

Baron-Cohen, S. (2004) The cognitive neuroscience of autism, *Journal of Neurology, Neurosurgery and Psychiatry*, 75(7): 945–8.

Bryan, K. (2004) Prevalence of speech and language difficulties in young offenders, *International Journal of Language and Communication Disorders*, 39(3): 391–400.

Cross, M. (2007) *Language and Social Exclusion*. London: I CAN. [Online.]

GOSH (2016) *Speech and Language Development from Birth to 12 Months*, Great Ormond Street Hospital for Children website. Available at: https://www.gosh.nhs.uk/medical-information-0/procedures-and-treatments/speech-and-language-development-birth-12-months (accessed 23 August 2020).

Gracia-Tabuenca, Z., Díaz-Patiño, J.C., Arelio, I. and Alcauter, S. (2020) Topological data analysis reveals robust alterations in the whole-brain and frontal lobe functional connectomes in attention-deficit/hyperactivity disorder, *eNeuro*, 7(3): ENEURO.0543-19.2020. doi: 10.1523/ENEURO.0543-19.2020. PMID: 32317343. PMCID: PMC7221355.

Mental Health First Aid England (MHFA) (2014) *Youth Mental Health in Education Manual*. London: MHFA.

NELFT (2009) *How Does a Child Develop Speech and Language?*, NELFT website. Available at: https://www.nelft.nhs.uk/services-havering-child-adolescent-salt-develop-speech-language/ (accessed 23 August 2020).

Qian, X., Castellanos, F.X., Uddin, L.Q., Loo, B.R.Y., Liu, S., Koh, H.L. et al. (2019) Large-scale brain functional network topology disruptions underlie symptom heterogeneity in children with attention-deficit/hyperactivity disorder, *Neuroimage Clinical*, 21. https://doi.org/10.1016/j.nicl.2018.11.010

Winstanley, C.A., Eagle, D.M. and Robbins, T.W. (2006) Behavioral models of impulsivity in relation to ADHD: translation between clinical and preclinical studies, *Clinical Psychology Review*, 26(4): 379–95.

6 Psychological factors: mental distress

Mental distress doesn't have to be indicative of a mental illness but instead suggests that an individual is experiencing challenges or changes that are having a negative impact on their mental health. Some of us reading this handbook may have experienced similar distress representing loss or change, but may have been more able to manage that distress. We may be able to express how we feel better and be able to draw upon the resources that we have around us.

We can see that there are an increasing number of childhood stressors, and this means an increase in the numbers of children exhibiting mental distress in the classroom. In understanding behaviour that may reveal mental distress we are likely to be in a better position to help those children and find ways to alleviate the distress. This is increasingly becoming a component of pastoral work in schools.

Mental distress may be caused by one or more of the following:

- exam pressure
- transitions
- bullying or negative peer relationships
- divorce
- bereavement
- arrival of a new sibling or step-parent
- moving home
- any other significant change.

Some individuals may find things on that list more distressing than others, and this is likely to be related to issues of self-esteem, what resources they have to draw on and how resilient they are. There is also the accumulative factor that several of the things on that list may occur, and it appears as if the child or young person is managing well, but the addition of something which may feel simple causes a more significant reaction. You may come across other things that are not on the list, but which may still have an effect on the child – they are just less frequently seen in the children we work with.

Children experiencing mental distress may feel:

- sad
- lonely
- confused

- anxious
- hopeless
- angry.

Some behaviours relating to mental distress include:

- disruption
- withdrawal
- tearfulness
- aggression
- running away from class
- hiding under tables
- destroying work
- lateness to school
- absence from school.

I will go into these in more detail, but while you are reading the case study of Alfie below see if you notice any of them. Many children experiencing mental distress during education are likely to be considered as having behavioural issues or forced to get a medical diagnosis to ensure they can get the support they need. Working in pupil referral unit settings that support children with medical needs taught me that it is important not to pathologize mental distress as mental illness. Here is the case study of Alfie who I worked with while he was dual-rolled at a PRU and mainstream school.

> Alfie was 8 years old, white British and from a single parent family. He had one older brother called David, who had special educational needs. Alfie initially attended a mainstream primary school before his behaviour become more difficult in the classroom. He would run away from teachers, hide under tables and in the morning would routinely be late as he was refusing to get dressed or be ready. His mum had started to bring him to school in his pyjamas as he was trying to avoid going to school at all. Alfie started throwing things at teachers when they approached too close. This escalated from just pens and paper to chairs and tables. After Alfie did this he would get really upset and cry. He would then ask to go home and write notes to say he was sorry for what happened. Alfie would need a lot of support to start a piece of work and sometimes would rip it up at the end. He would also rip other children's work off the wall, further upsetting them. Alfie would not play with other children and used to sit in or wander around the playground on his own.
>
> While attending the PRU for children at risk of exclusion, Alfie would behave in a similar way. He would hide under the foyer chairs and have to be coaxed out. But Alfie could often be easily distracted from this initial behaviour if you caught him quickly and talked about his pet cats, which he loved.

Psychological factors: mental distress   65

Figure 6.1 Five stages of responding

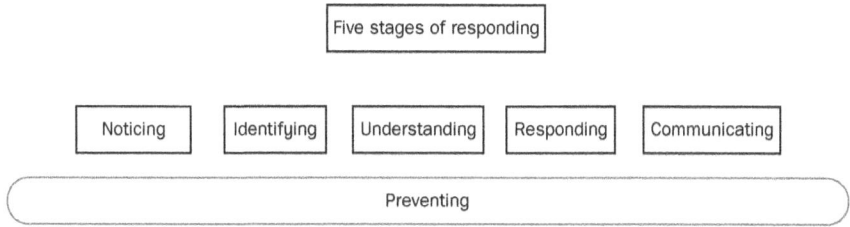

There were a number of things I didn't initially know about Alfie. I knew he loved cats, and had three himself, but it wasn't until I went to his house that his mum told me she used to hold a yearly stall to raise funds to rescue them. Nor did I know that his difficult behaviour happened at the time his big brother David was sectioned under the Mental Health Act and spent some time receiving care outside the home in a psychiatric unit. It was the first time that David (who was 15 at the time) had left the home. I discovered this when I visited Alfie and his mum at home after a serious incident where Alfie had attempted to harm himself by tying a skipping rope around his neck and telling me that he wanted to die.

As teachers, there are a number of things we may *notice* in Alfie's behaviour:

- hiding under tables
- throwing things
- wandering on his own
- tearfulness.

We could *identify* that he is:

- upset
- scared.

Only after finding out more about Alfie's mental distress do we begin to understand what is potentially causing his behaviour. Whilst above I have repeated the Five stages of responding figure, below I help to guide through this process by unpicking some of the behaviours he presented, with the formulation of mental distress as an underpinning factor that drives the behaviour.

Alfie was in mental distress. He had seen his older brother David being taken away in an ambulance, and then he did not return for some time as he was admitted to hospital a significant distance from the family home. Given Alfie's young age, his mum had been honest in saying that David was feeling poorly and had gone to hospital, but was not able to say when he would return home. So Alfie was suffering, for all intents and purposes, a loss. He had lost his brother for a period of time and didn't know when he would come back. Moreover, Alfie didn't have the words to express how he was feeling. Much of his behaviour was driven by the desire to be sent home and be with his mum. He had learned that behaving in increasingly difficult ways meant that the headteacher felt she had little choice in making that decision by issuing a fixed-term exclusion.

- **Disruptive behaviours**

  Some of the things that Alfie demonstrates above can be seen as disruptive behaviour. You may hear some of these behaviours being called 'attention seeking'. From a wider perspective they may include not following the teacher's instructions, or intentionally behaving in ways that are seen as 'silly' or infantile. Disruptive behaviours are things that interrupt the teaching and learning of others. They can be really difficult to manage, but in understanding that in this instance with Alfie it was about his mental distress, we can see that there are other ways we may respond to support his difficulties. For Alfie, he knew that if he behaved in some of the ways described above he would be sent home to 'cool off' – or what his mum knew as a fixed-term exclusion. He wasn't just worried about his brother; he was worried that his mum would go to hospital one day too. In his own mind, Alfie was doing what a good boy should do: looking after his mum.

- **Withdrawal**

  This may be seen as children and young people avoiding engaging in group activity or going out into the playground. You might see these children preferring sitting on their own, or eating their lunch somewhere else. It may be because they don't feel important or don't think others will miss them, and being on their own has fewer social demands than trying to explain how they feel. Withdrawal is often tied in with self-esteem: 'Why would Jacob want to be with me? I am boring anyway.' We can see how self-talk or the inner voice has a part to play in a child's external behaviour, as well as being distressing internally.

- **Tearfulness**

  Obviously some children and young people have a lower threshold to becoming tearful than others, and you may notice a child who cries for no apparent reason and becomes visibly upset. Alfie would often demonstrate his mental distress after an event by crying. Some of this relates to the effect of being in a high arousal state, and you might see it in children you work with. But Alfie also felt incredibly guilty, knowing his mum would have to come and get him when she had so much else to do. And as he didn't have the words to express this guilt it came out in tears.

- **Aggression**

  A child may have a low threshold to things being changed, but not have the words to express how they are feeling. This may be displayed in anger and aggression towards others. Alfie's frustration at not being able to express how he felt was linked to his anger about what had happened to his brother. For him, aggression was a mechanism which meant he could look after his mum, who he was worried about. I would suggest that a number of factors led to Alfie's aggressive outbursts. I also wondered whether Alfie, after seeing his brother taken by ambulance from the family home, worried that one day this might also happen to him.

- **Running away from class**
  A child may wish to avoid the classroom space, and – rather than being aggressive – will run away to seek safety. Here, the fight or flight response kicks in. Again, this is something we see with Alfie, who frequently runs away from the class.
- **Hiding under tables**
  Similar to running away, some children respond to mental distress by hiding in different spaces in the classroom. For some, if one is available, it may be a safety tent; for others, it may be by hiding under a table or behind a door, or somewhere else in the classroom that is away from other children.
- **Destroying work**
  As noted above, Alfie would frequently rip up his work. For some, this may be a way of self-jeopardizing, where a child has done something well but they don't want others to see it. Or they may not see their work as being good, and rip it up in their own frustration. Some children may see their first piece of work as a draft, and be relaxed about it; but others require immediate gratification, and see a piece of work as just another example of something that has gone wrong.
- **Lateness**
  There are various reasons for a child coming to school late. They may be avoiding the school space and be arguing with parents/carers about attending. They may have found it difficult to organize themselves and missed the bus. Or they may have found it hard to get to sleep the night before because they were worrying about something else. For Alfie, it was a way of trying to increase the time he spent with his mum – if he could be at home then maybe he could make sure she was ok.
- **Absence from school**
  You may notice that some children in mental distress are frequently absent from school. These children can be driven by a way of seeing home as somewhere safe and nurturing and so staying at home is a way of demonstrating risk aversion. Some children may be worried (and not in the context of an anxiety disorder) and have stomach aches or headaches that are also driving their absence from school.

Mental distress and the signs of someone being upset, sad or finding things hard, does not need to be diagnosed or pathologized. There may not need to be a specific intervention in helping children like Alfie, but in developing an understanding about what is driving some of the things that we see externally we may be able to add up the clues to what is happening internally. In finding out more about Alfie, it was noticing his behaviours that helped me understand – talking to his mum, finding out more about what was going on for him at home, and seeing the wider situation for his home and family.

7 Understanding psychological factors: mental illness

In understanding psychological factors relating to mental health we need to understand and define the difference between mental illness and risks to your mental health. Figure 7.1 provides a good starting point to consider some of the differences that may help us understand the factors that can influence our mental health.

The implication of this in education is that often while we focus on one aspect, we oversimplify the complexity of what drives behaviour. It is incredibly rare to find a behaviour that can be stripped down to just one factor. However, you often see behavioural policies in the schooling environment that embrace one particular approach and ignore others. This puts us in the precarious position of not being able to fully understand a range of needs we may observe in the classroom, trapped in our overall approach and ultimately unable to provide nuanced personalized support for the children in our care.

In approaching from one perspective we are also in danger of not being able to narrate what we see effectively. If we are driven by ideas that mental illness is just caused by loss, or is just a sign of normal adolescence, we can find it difficult to articulate why we may want further support to help children. Or we may rely on ill-fitting responses, such as isolating a child when they are already suffering from isolation as a factor in their behavioural responses.

In the education system there have been increasing concerns about the mental health of our children. There have been worries about family structures, use of social networking sites and children's resilience to manage what is happening in the wider context. Having worked as the teacher-in-charge of the education department of a psychiatric system, I supported the education of children who were receiving treatment within a Tier 4 service. This service was developed for children who had severe and enduring mental health needs. The children were aged 12 to 18, and their needs were varied, with diagnoses such as anorexia nervosa, psychosis, obsessive compulsive disorder and post-traumatic stress disorder.

In the context of this clinical setting, a formulation and understanding is created from the advice given by psychiatrists, pharmacists, family therapists, psychologists, occupational therapists and the education team. This whole team provided a richness of approach, and mental illness and mental health was seen in a wider biological, psychological and situational context.

It is interesting to note that many of these interventions and forms of support, which would also benefit children early on in the school setting, frequently

Figure 7.1 Mental illness

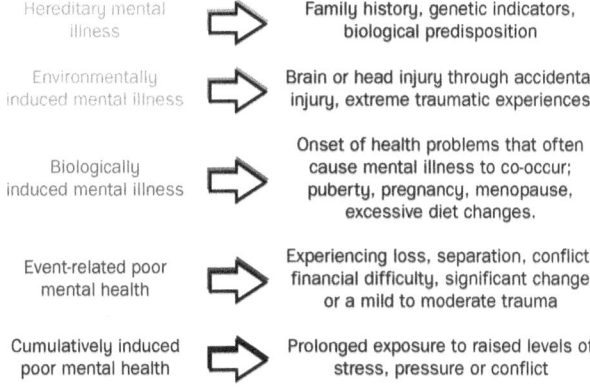

occur in psychiatric inpatient services but due to access to resources are not part of the general support.

This chapter moves beyond noticing to understanding the drivers behind certain behaviours. In the context of mental illness I have focused on a number of children, including Jason, who was diagnosed with schizophrenia. I begin with him as there is a significant stigma associated with schizophrenia, but I also talk about Aashirya (OCD), Avia (anorexia nervosa), Peter (clinical depression) and Fariq (bipolar disorder), to provide a snapshot of their behaviours and understand them on a deeper level, to be able to respond to their needs as outlined in later chapters.

Schizophrenia

Jason had been initially diagnosed as having psychosis, but after several episodes of being unwell, this was changed to schizophrenia. Essentially, the *noticing* has been done, so now we need to consider how we understand this behaviour and why it exists.

> Jason was a 15-year-old boy with a diagnosis of schizophrenia. He was attending school before admission into Tier 4 psychiatric services, but his behaviour became more bizarre and unmanageable both at school and in the wider community. Jason would shout at people in the street, talk to pigeons and ride buses around the city for long hours. His mum became increasingly concerned about his well-being and there would be many arguments in the family home. Jason would start to accuse his mum of poisoning his food and he began to lose weight. In being admitted to a psychiatric unit there was an opportunity for the multidisciplinary team to speak to his schoolteachers to

find out how he was at school. A history was provided by his teachers which reported that Jason had been issued several fixed-term exclusions for persistent disruptive behaviour. Jason would walk in and out of the classroom – and not necessarily classes he was expected to attend. He would attempt to talk to some of the other children in the class, frequently run out of class and hide in cupboards, and say that other children were bullying him. Jason would screech, make random noises and interrupt the learning of others.

Jason attended education in the psychiatric unit and presented as disorganized, distracted and generally unfocused. While in a smaller environment, his behaviour was similar, albeit more manageable.

One afternoon I was teaching Jason. As a class we were reading *Roll of Thunder, Hear My Cry*, and while another child was reading, Jason interrupted, shouting and standing up animatedly from his seat. 'What the fuck is that outside?' Turning around I looked out of the window in the direction Jason was pointing. Nothing was outside. Jason continued, 'Oh my god it's a clown shitting!' The other children laughed, and I initially thought he was trying to disrupt the lesson. But then I realized Jason looked scared.

I said, 'Oh Jason, that must be really worrying. But there is no clown outside. Let's carry on with reading. Can you read this out loud for me?' He looked at me and I pointed in the book to where he should continue reading out loud in order to refocus him. As he settled I said, 'If you need to pop outside of the class, then just come back in a few moments'.

Jason struggled to return to school. There was a lot of support around focused transition which included shorter days, a place where he could go to if he felt unsafe and a check in and check out with a teacher. However, despite Jason finding things really difficult, he did eventually attend school full-time and even took his GCSEs the following year (he liked science in particular).

With Jason, it was really hard not to notice his behaviour. The key characteristics were that he was:

- disruptive
- agitated
- scared
- angry.

Below, I look at ways of developing an understanding of these behaviours in the context of his diagnosis of schizophrenia. For clinical settings, this may be seen as a formulation, but I am mindful of my role as a teacher – and while I have enjoyed the experience of being in a psychiatric unit and have learned lots, my role is about understanding these behaviours through the lens of teaching and developing a conducive classroom and schooling environment.

I will start with a brief overview of some of the diagnostic symptoms of schizophrenia and then apply them to understanding Jason's behaviour. In writing this section, in keeping with my belief that those with lived experiences are the real experts, I asked a friend with the same diagnosis to 'sense check' the information.

Those with a diagnosis of schizophrenia have two or more of these symptoms (American Psychiatric Association, 2013):

1 Delusions – a strong belief in something there is no evidence for, does not sit within a cultural understanding and is refuted by rational argument. For example, I have worked with a child who believed he had a chip in his brain, and another who thought his eyes belonged to the rapper Tupac.
2 Hallucinations – seeing or experiencing things that other people may not see, smell or fear.
3 Disorganized speech – easily distracted from what they are trying to say. It may be that it is hard to follow a topic or the meaning the person is trying to make clear.
4 Disorganized or catatonic behaviour – you might see that a child has difficulty doing a set task. For example, packing their bags or getting dressed for school may become a very difficult task as the organization becomes mixed up or slow.
5 Negative symptoms – seemingly blank, monotone and not really engaging with what is around them.

Disruptive

As already mentioned, Jason was incredibly disruptive in school – walking in and out of class, shouting at people, jumping out of cupboards where he had been hiding. It is easy to see that if we remain on the first step of the five-stage formula – 'noticing' – that Jason clearly required a fixed-term exclusion for his behaviour. However, if we look at the next stage, 'understanding', we can see that fixed-term exclusions are not an appropriate way to respond to or prevent his behaviour. Jason's disruptive behaviour was driven by his fear. Jason experienced things that other people were not privy to. For example, his exclamation 'What the fuck is that outside? Oh my god it's a clown shitting!' can simply be seen as disruption, but if we add the stage of *understanding* that Jason is hallucinating – in this instance, experiencing things that we do not see – then seeing this in the context of mere 'disruption' shows that we have not truly understood what is driving this behaviour. Hallucinations can be incredibly frightening. For some, they may be comforting and humorous; but for Jason, seeing a clown defecating in the space outside his classroom was frightening and upsetting. His reaction – to tell his peers and his teachers – if using the lens of understanding, is actually about him trying to warn those around him of something that could be harmful and threatening, not just to himself but to others.

Agitated

Jason's behaviour was often described as agitated. He would find it difficult to settle in class, be up and down in his seat, and fiddle with things like his trouser leg, tie and shirt. As already mentioned, Jason would also hide in cupboards and jump out unexpectedly. If we return to two symptoms of schizophrenia – hallucinations and disorganized behaviour – we can understand more about the driving factors behind these behaviours. His believing that there were strange things around him, or that he was being bullied by others – and he may well have been, in that children may have noticed his increasingly bizarre behaviour, but not have understood what was causing it – drove his behaviour to hide away from those who were upsetting him, real or imagined. Hiding was Jason's escape mechanism.

Disorganized behaviour is a more complex aspect of schizophrenia. Here, the behaviour of an individual can fluctuate from excessive movements to freezing in place. Jason's fiddling with his school clothes could be driven by thoughts (although Jason did not tell us) or by virtue of the realities of schizophrenia. With Jason, this agitation was furthered when there were aspects around an incoherency in understanding what he was trying to say. Sometimes, people with schizophrenia may be wrestling with the distraction of voices talking to them. These may be derogatory in nature, saying frightening, unkind or threatening things. Imagine trying to sustain a conversation when there are competing voices outside of your conversation saying things about you. These are very difficult to filter out, and make it a real struggle to focus on a conversation. Knowing all of this deepens our understanding of Jason's behaviour and helps us avoid simply seeing his behaviour as 'persistently disruptive'. We understand it more as Jason grappling with a range of stimuli that is difficult for him to manage.

Anorexia nervosa

Anorexia nervosa is an incredibly complicated psychiatric illness caused by a whole range of factors. You may wish to understand anorexia nervosa from a psychiatric, psychological or neurological perspective, and for this I encourage you to review current literature and articles associated with this condition. Here, I focus on understanding what we may notice in the classroom setting for later stages of support in our schooling environments. Some key features of anorexia nervosa include:

1 intentionally missing meals or restricting your dietary intake to avoid eating foods that are seen as fattening
2 believing that you are fat when you are a healthy weight or underweight
3 using medication to suppress your appetite.

Sadly, anorexia has the highest death rate associated with mental illness. While for some children the high mortality rate is due to the significant physical implications of limiting their energy intake, for others it is due to suicide (Arcelus et al., 2011). To understand anorexia nervosa from the perspective of a teacher I have explored Avia and her behaviour.

Understanding psychological factors: mental illness **73**

> Avia was admitted to the psychiatric inpatient service on three occasions in the period I worked there. At the time she was 15 years old, and was white European, having emigrated from one of the Baltic states when she was 10 years old. When I first met Avia she was unable to come to the classroom; her weight was too low and her activities and movements were very restricted. She began a refeeding programme with the aim of stabilizing her physical symptoms. This was a long process. Avia initially used a nasal gastric tube as she was too distressed to physically eat. After a while she started coming to the classroom. Her English was perfect and she spoke slowly and carefully. Avia was particularly interested in completing any work from her home school, which she had not attended for several months prior to admission to the inpatient service. She refused to engage in the other activities in the classroom that were intended to supplement her schoolwork, telling me quite clearly that they were pointless.

Avia would not talk much to me, but the key characteristics were that she was:

- agitated
- angry
- argumentative.

As always, it is important to recognize that the diagnosis does not necessarily indicate the later behaviours, but if we use the diagnosis as a lens to understand Avia's presentation in her class it puts us in a better position to be able to help her.

Agitated

Avia would often arrive late to class, meaning that she did not get to participate in setting the tone of the lesson or reiteration of the focus. Her lateness was caused by a strict feeding regime which was punctuated by her own distress (and probably the distress of staff) and therefore elongated the whole process. When Avia eventually came to class she would not sit down immediately. Instead she walked back and forth to get her book, which she could have done in one walk. Or, if the book was already on the table, she would stand awkwardly behind the chair. I have seen this behaviour in other children with anorexia nervosa, and it is often due to an intense desire or compulsion to maximize physical activity and lose weight. It can also be due to the stress and fear of thinking about the next meal, or the calories they have just eaten.

Angry

Avia would often present as being quite angry. She did not like being asked to sit down or to complete certain work. I would characterize our relationship as poor (I am not sure how she felt about me, but she was often quite dismissive, annoyed or angry with me, so I think she would say the same thing!) Anorexia nervosa is driven by a need to be in control, and being in an inpatient hospital means that a lot of the control you are normally able to assert is stripped away. It is stripped away with the legal discourse of being sectioned under the Mental Health Act; and the very thing that most of us have a choice about – what we put in our mouths – is also taken away. There is also the aspect of anxiety here – being anxious about putting on weight and then being at heightened arousal has the real potential of making an individual feel traumatized and, as with anyone when presented with a threat, resorting to flight or fight. I had frequent verbal fights with Avia, but I believe these were not just due to frustration with me as an individual, but because she felt anxious about her particular circumstances.

Obsessive compulsive disorder

I want to build upon how some specific behaviours we may witness in the classroom and school environment help us to understand obsessive compulsive disorder.

> Aashirya liked to be known by the shortened form of Aash. Aash was 14 years old when I first met her and was from the Bengali community. She had one older brother who was married and living in the family home. They had a positive relationship with one another and spent time playing board games and going to gigs. Aash enjoyed music, especially alternative rock. However, as she became increasingly unwell she spent more time indoors, her school attendance significantly decreased, then she stopped going altogether. She would spend a number of hours in the morning applying make-up – thick eyeliner, dark eyeshadow and bright red lipstick. While she was still attending school, Aash would arrive late as she had a number of compulsive rituals that she had to perform before leaving the house. But one of these – using make-up – was against the school rules. Aash would often be late to classes as she had to go through a cycle of walking to the next class a number of times. Her teachers reported seeing her looking at her reflection in windows and compulsively walking backwards and forwards. When Aash did come to class she would stand for several minutes before sitting down, and then be unable to pick up her pen. She appeared constantly distracted, even in quiet classrooms.

The key characteristics were that Aash was:

- distracted
- late.

Distracted

In keeping with Aash's diagnosis of OCD, she had a number of intrusive thoughts which were distressing and threatening. These were sometimes belittling negative words or phrases or, more often, seeing the image of her brother injured after traumatic accidents. While Aash's teachers noticed that she often appeared distracted in class, they didn't necessarily realize that her internal world was being subsumed by these thoughts. Aash found it harder to concentrate on what she was meant to be doing. Part of this was due to reoccurring distressing images of her brother, while the other aspect was the internal compulsion of counting and making sure she didn't miss a number that would result in her brother's death. She would have to be told on a number of occasions to refocus and do her work. In understanding these driving factors we can also see this in the context of explaining Aash's lateness.

Arriving late

In order to prevent seeing her brother's injured and lifeless body Aash had begun to count how many times she would see herself during the day. She would always have to finish on an odd number, otherwise she felt that her brother would end up horribly injured. Her teachers noticed her continual lateness, but didn't understand that this was due to a strategy of ensuring her brother did not get hurt.

Clinical depression

We are all vulnerable to feeling sad, low and hopeless at times. Life rarely goes as smoothly as we would like, and these feelings may be entirely in context of what is happening around us. Clinical depression is an extension of these feelings, and some of the symptoms are:

- a continuous low mood or sadness
- feelings of being helpless
- feelings of hopelessness
- being tearful
- irritability and a low tolerance of other people
- lack of motivation or interest in things that may have previously been something you enjoyed
- feelings of anxiety
- thoughts of self-harm or ending your life (American Psychiatric Association, 2013).

In terms of understanding this behaviour in school, I have focused on Peter.

> Peter was 13 years old and in year 9 at school when he first tried to kill himself. He was from a white middle-class family and attended a grammar school after passing his 11 Plus exam. Peter's upbringing appeared fairly typical and he had an older sister. His school attendance was excellent and he was interested in a range of subjects, particularly maths and science. Peter was struggling to choose his GCSE subjects for the following year, and when his teacher asked why he replied, 'I don't know what I want to do'. Peter stopped going to rugby club after school, and would not contribute to class groupwork, instead working on his own. He stopped answering teachers' questions in class unless directly called upon. Peter was always polite, but became quieter, spending an increasing amount of time on his own. One Friday after school, Peter returned to his empty form classroom and attempted to hang himself. Fortunately he was discovered by the cleaner, and an ambulance was called.

The key characteristics were that Peter was:

- quiet
- withdrawn.

Below, I develop a further understanding of Peter by considering his behaviour through using the framework of depression.

Quiet

One of the key symptoms of depression is low mood and feelings of hopelessness and helplessness. Peter stopped engaging in groupwork and seemed to prefer to be on his own. He also stopped answering questions in class. We could see this behaviour as being driven by a general lack of interest in relation to being depressed. It is hard to want to engage in a class when you feel hopeless and are unable to really feel any purpose. This is especially so in the case of Peter, who was unable to choose his GCSE subjects. This is a key component of understanding why Peter presented as being withdrawn.

Withdrawn

Peter's lack of motivation relating to depression meant that he further and further isolated himself from his peers. He had less of an interest in being with people around him. This in turn is likely to have influenced the way that he felt about himself and his self-esteem. Being clinically depressed meant Peter started to disengage from future plans – he wasn't able to choose his GCSEs, not just because he had a lack of focus but because there was a sense of 'there's no point'. In class, you may see that a child like Peter stops wanting to spend time with friends, may cancel things that they otherwise enjoyed, and they become more and more insular. In turn, other children may find the poverty of thought and speech (lack of talking, slowing of thoughts) difficult to engage with and further drift away.

Bipolar disorder

Bipolar disorder is not as frequently seen as some of the mental illnesses in this chapter, but can cause significantly difficulties in terms of how children may present in the classroom. I describe bipolar, as although we may associate it more with older people, it most often begins to present itself during adolescence. Bipolar is classed as a mood disorder in the *Diagnostic and Statistical Manual of Mental Disorders* (DSM), where six different types of bipolar are detailed. Some key symptoms are outlined below:

- an inflated sense of self-esteem or being grandiose
- not needing as much sleep
- more talkative or feels a pressure to keep talking, may have fast paced speech
- may describe their thoughts as racing
- easily distractible
- excessive engagement in pleasurable activities that may be risky (such as sex, or drug taking may be a particular concern) (American Psychiatric Association, 2013).
- depression

To develop our understanding beyond a focus on symptoms, I have outlined the case of Fariq.

> Fariq is 16 years old and is a British born, second generation Indian from a middle-class family. His mother is a solicitor and his father works in the car industry. Fariq attends the local school and works hard, but more recently his teachers have noticed that he has been losing his temper with his friends and getting into fights. He has also got into arguments with teachers and has not been completing work. Fariq has complained that he is finding it difficult to sleep and appears tired. He is quick to interrupt as well as offer answers in class. He has received several fixed-term exclusions for persistent disruptive behaviour, but of late has received a three-day exclusion for verbal abuse to a peer. Fariq has begun to truant from school and has said that he might as well not bother going to school if he is going to be suspended, and anyway he has decided that he is going to open up his own boxing gym. Fariq's mum has expressed concerns that he is out too often and smoking drugs, which she understands to be cannabis. Fariq has also started messaging a girl on both Instagram and Snapchat, and sending pictures of his penis to her. His mum has confiscated his phone but Fariq has just said he will get another one and doesn't care. In a back-to-school meeting with the headteacher after one fixed-term exclusion, Fariq told her to fuck off and pushed a chair over before leaving the school site.

Some of the behaviours that Fariq demonstrates as a response to bipolar disorder are:

- argumentativeness
- aggression
- truanting.

Argumentativeness

A number of symptoms of bipolar disorder feed into understanding why Fariq may seem argumentative to others. If you consider that Fariq may have racing thoughts as well as being grandiose, he may be finding it difficult to understand why he is being told to do something by a teacher, or anyone else for that matter. In addition, he may have what is often described as 'pressure of speech', which is talking rapidly and not always making much sense that someone else can follow. Especially for other children or adults who may not understand why Fariq is continually talking over them, you can see how this may be seen as argumentative and quite a difficult behaviour to support in the school setting.

Aggression

Fariq's behaviour may be described as aggressive in terms of pushing over the chair as well as sending pictures of his genitalia to a girl on social networking sites. Again, drawing this back to our understanding of bipolar disorder, we can see how some of his difficulties have arisen from the inflated self-esteem and racing thoughts. Normally, you might find that a child would consider the consequences of being rude to a member of staff (especially a headteacher) and worry about how a sexual picture may be received by others. However in Fariq's case, this 'stop' to what may be his normal, typical behaviour does not feature.

Truanting

Fariq has expressed in the case study how he doesn't see the point of education as he has alternative plans in opening a boxing gym. He has also been smoking cannabis, which may have had an impact on his motivation and engagement. In this presentation of bipolar, Fariq is struggling with an impulsive desire, which is perhaps a reflection of hubris, to open his own boxing gym as well as with others telling him what to do. When we place his behaviour in this context and understand it through the lens of bipolar, it comes as no surprise that Fariq is behaving in the way that he is.

References

American Psychiatric Association (2013) *Diagnosis and Statistical Manual of Mental Disorders*, 5th edition: DSM-5. Arlington, VA: American Psychiatric Association.

Arcelus, J., Mitchell, A.J., Wales. J. and Nielsen, S. (2011) Mortality rates in patients with anorexia nervosa and other eating disorders: a meta-analysis of 36 studies, *Archives of General Psychiatry*, 68(7): 724–31. doi:10.1001/archgenpsychiatry.2011.74

8 Understanding mental diversity

Not every child you meet who presents with behaviours that you could describe as 'disruptive' or 'challenging' will have underlying mental health problems, vulnerabilities or unmet needs. There are times when some children and young people demonstrate a preference for different environments, or act in ways that we find surprising or unexpected. Sometimes children are bored and want to 'liven things up' in the classroom. It does not mean that they have an unmet need, but may want to have fun and this is how they think they will achieve it. It may be that our interactions with the child are driving some of the behaviours that we see in the classroom, and this too should be reflected on.

Ask yourself before you intervene, respond and engage: 'does it really matter?' Now, your school may be setting a specific culture of support, and it is important that you don't ignore things that could make another staff member vulnerable if they follow up a school rule and you don't. 'Well Mrs Dove didn't say anything about me wearing make-up' can lead to a whole host of issues and difficulties if you have been permissive and not factored in the school culture. I am thinking more of other things that may be seen as low-level disruption – ask yourself if the tapping of the pen really matters? Does it matter if the child hums as they are focusing on a maths problem? Does their action distress others? Is it distressing or damaging to them as an individual? Do they even realize they are doing it? Instead, think about how we can embrace that child's preference. How can we show that we accept their difference and facilitate it?

There are certain phrases in behavioural management strategies such as taking pride that a school '*sweats the small stuff*': really focusing on low-level disruption to ensure that it does not get out of hand. Some of this stems from sociological perspectives such as the Broken Window theory (Wilson and Kelling, 1998). This theory built upon the idea that very minor things in the community (such as a broken window, small pieces of graffiti) if left untouched would invite further disorder and would escalate towards serious crime. You can see how this may be understood and generalized in the schooling setting (Ashman, 2015; Bennett, 2016), and indeed Bennett in particular offers some important points about noticing what may seem minor behaviour and trying to understand what it may mean. However, when talking about 'sweating the small stuff' there is also the balance of seeing some behaviours as just a consequence of the diversity of individuals.

In trying to understand mental diversity think about the alternative of responding to the event or perceived infraction. What would be the impact on that child, you as a teacher and the wider school community? In discussing this, I will briefly focus on Daniel.

> Daniel is 11 years old, a white British boy living in a single parent family with his mum and his grandmother. He has recently moved from primary to secondary school and is one of the younger children in his year. In moving up to his secondary school a number of his friends also moved up class. Whenever Daniel is working he hums – you are not sure if he even notices it.

Now there are different approaches that we may take for Daniel. We should definitely think about what may be driving this behaviour and ask ourselves questions that may help us understand, but it may be that humming is just that, humming. We could decide to ask him to stop, and when he doesn't (because it is habitual), escalate to further interventions (we may label it as persistent disruptive behaviour) and send him out of the class and so on. We could, in the words of some, 'sweat the small stuff'. Or we could see this as just the way that Daniel works. We may even wish to investigate further; a telephone to his primary school would quickly tell us whether or not Daniel has always hummed when he is concentrating, or if this is a new thing that is perhaps a sign of distress and upset.

If we are to consider the impact of not working in the ways that suit Daniel, we can perhaps see that he might find it difficult to concentrate in class, or that if he cannot hum he will feel uncomfortable or awkward. In a different scenario, even if a child wants to sit nearer to the window rather than the door or in the middle of the class but this won't fit with your seating plan, I would suggest just acknowledging that all children are different and may have particular preferences – this is no different from an adult who likes to sit by the phone in the office or in the corner.

If we then follow Daniel's potential journey and the impact of attempting to stop him humming and to shape him within specific rules of the school, we can perhaps see an escalation of behaviour without even finding out if this is just what Daniel does.

In Figure 8.1 we can see how there is an escalation of things from the initial behaviour. When we talk about sweating the small stuff, yes it may be important to identify and understand some of the behaviours that we see in order to build in an appropriate response. Equally it is important to just ask yourself 'is what I am seeing just how someone is?'

While this child may not suffer from systematic prejudice such as we may see in racism or patriarchy, he is being focused upon because of an external behaviour that is likely to have little effect on others. Of course we need to be considerate of the other children in our class and how they may interpret his behaviour, but there is also a sense that we need to develop and build systems that are supportive of mutual reciprocity, where all children feel like they belong despite not responding or being the same as the child next to them.

82 Understanding

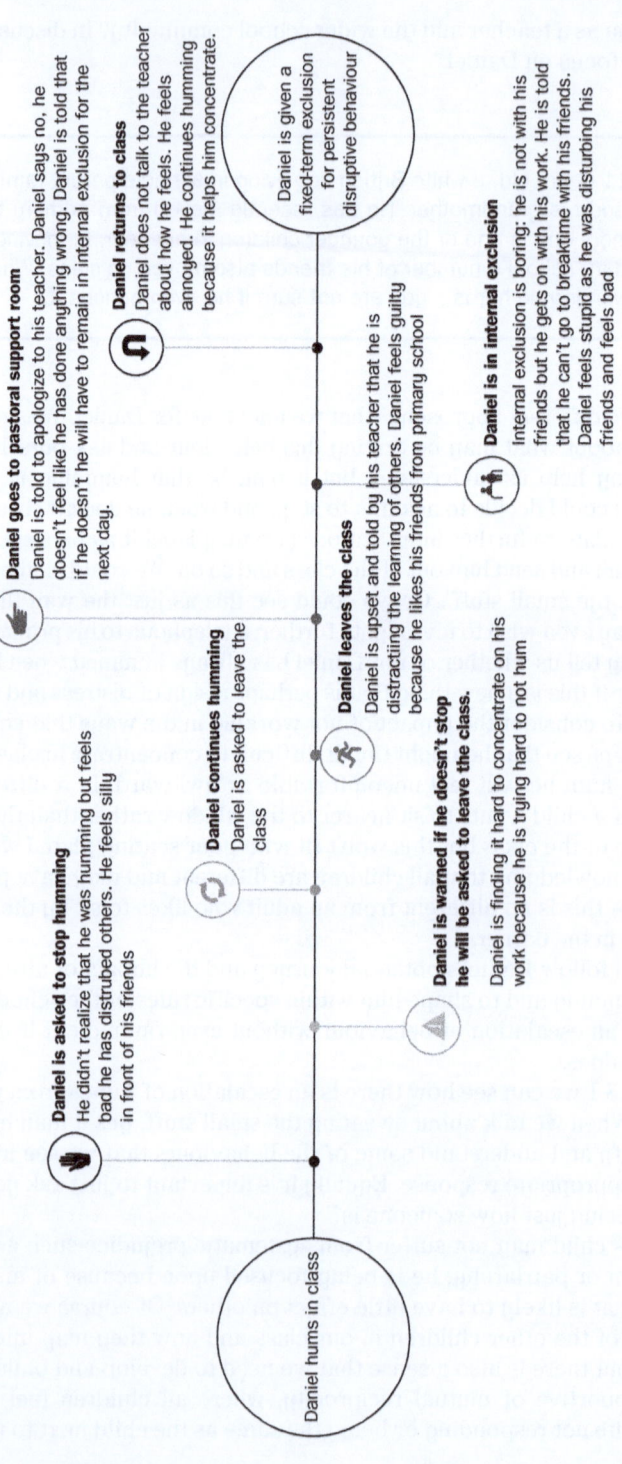

Figure 8.1 Daniel's journey towards a fixed-term exclusion

In Daniel's journey towards fixed-term exclusion he was asked to leave the room and this is a particular moment in Daniel's story where he is told, in no uncertain terms, that his behaviour will not be tolerated, isn't appropriate and is not welcomed in the classroom.

In my own research into children's experiences of alternative provision, a recurring theme was that of belonging, how children experience and feel like they are part of a community. While Daniel may have initially felt like he was part of a community, in being asked to leave and going to internal isolation, a message is sent that the way that he exhibits a behaviour that he may have done for many years is not welcomed. Moreover, the lack of a conversation with the teacher before he returned to class places both teacher and pupil in a difficult position where there is unresolved tension.

I wonder when we think about mental diversity, how do we create equality in regards to our neurological preferences and needs? How do we facilitate diversity, beyond that of protected characteristics, to consider how we communicate, what helps us focus, what motivates us and how we enjoy and engage in rewards and recognitions?

In Daniel's case there were a number of missed opportunities, moments where professional curiosity could have been engaged which would probably have brought about a quiet acceptance of understanding that this is how Daniel is. It is not about not having high expectations of Daniel; it is about not limiting Daniel because of our thoughts and requirements for children, causing them to behave in stifled ways. We are all in a remarkable position where we can change the outcome of Daniel's story, and it doesn't have to be difficult, time-consuming or costly. It can just be about asking the right questions at the right time – 'Daniel, do you realize that you hum when you are working?' – and being curious to develop a real understanding that sometimes children just behave in ways that aren't the same as us, or the child sitting next to them.

References

Ashman, G. (2015) *Behaviour – For Great Rewards Sweat the Small Stuff*, TES website. Available at: https://www.tes.com/news/behaviour-great-rewards-sweat-small-stuff (accessed 5 June 2020).

Bennett, T. (2016) *Do Sweat the Small Stuff (for the Sake of your Students)*, TES website. Available at: https://www.tes.com/news/do-sweat-small-stuff-sake-your-students (accessed 23 August 2020)

Wilson, J.Q. and Kelling, G.L. (1998) Broken windows: the police and neighborhood safety, in G.F. Cole and M.G. Gertz (eds) *The Criminal Justice System: Politics and Policies*, 7th edn. Belmont, CA: Wadsworth Publishing, pp. 103–15.

9 Recognizing relationships

Relationships are a key feature of a person's life. The relationships we have with those around us can have a fundamental impact on how we behave, how we understand the world around us and how we respond to events and others. Relationships are powerful: they can make children feel safe or threatened, vulnerable or proud. I have seen relationships make a difference to how children respond in class and how they take risks in approaching a task. Relationships can steer a lesson in a way that you may least expect. This section is given over to this core but often under-discussed area of teaching practice, and to looking at different ideas around relationships and how we might understand how relationships can have such an effect.

Just like behaviour is complex, so too are the relationships that we have and how we experience them. We have discussed previously considerations around attachment theory and how that may underpin certain attachment styles, but there is also the understanding that relationships shift and change.

When we become teachers we recognize the importance of understanding the curriculum and key pedagogical issues. These are vital, but so too are relationships – not just between the teacher and pupil, but the relationship between parents and child, wider family, the local community and how a child feels they belong to the wider school community. In recognizing relationships and the impact they may have on a child's behaviour, we gain a further critical understanding of what is happening underneath the layers of complex behaviour we may see.

In order to understand the impact that relationships can have on a child's behaviour, I start by looking broadly at the often polarized debates around 'nature versus nurture', before reviewing social learning theory and considering attachment and how this may present in terms of behaviour.

Nature or nurture?

There has been a lot of debate around this subject over the years, and I won't labour the point, which will ultimately conclude that it is nuanced and everyone is different. However, I would be amiss if I didn't explore some key factors that may link into pedagogy and presenting behaviours. If this is a subject of particular interest, I encourage you to look at the references at the end of this chapter and follow it up in more depth.

Figure 9.1 Nature vs nurture

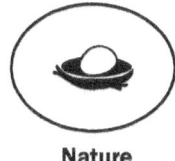

Nature

A child's behaviour is influenced largely by genetic factors

Nurture

A child develops key features of their behaviour through interaction with their environment and the relationships they have

You are likely to have heard key ideas relating to the nature versus nurture debate, which aims to ascertain how much of particular aspects of behaviour are inherited genetically or learned through the various influences in our lives. If we consider behaviour, nature is what we might see as pre-existing and determined largely by things that as teachers we can do little to influence. On the other hand nurture is the effect of the influence of external factors, things that are developed and learned. This debate is concerned with the contribution of each of these, and how this may shape human behaviour.

In Chapter 2, 'Identifying: correlation with known conditions', we looked specifically at attachment theory and how we may notice some behaviours of children we work with that can be driven by secure or insecure attachments. In developing this idea we may look at ways in which we can attempt to address what is seen as poor attachment, or interventions such as nurture groups. Ofsted (2011) reviews nurture groups and highlights how the intervention is based on the development of relationships with an adult:

> They aim to provide a predictable environment in which pupils can build trusting relationships with adults and gain the skills they need to learn in larger classes. (Ofsted, 2011: 4)

We can note that this approach takes a focus on developing a child's emotional well-being by framing an understanding that children have missed the development of key relationships in various ways. The aim of these groups is to model positive adult to child relationships, develop those beyond the school gate and provide strategies for children to be able to manage behaviours that have presented as difficult in the classroom or school environment.

Social learning theory influences this idea that modelling behaviour can help children copy and generalize strategies in their own lives. Social learning theory, proposed by Bandura (1973), offers an alternative to the polarized nature versus nurture debate. Instead, social learning theory attempts to explain human behaviour in terms of the interplay between cognition (how we think), behaviour (what we do) and environmental factors.

Social learning theory identifies particular conditions that are necessary to support a child's behaviour:

- attention (how much attention is being paid to what is being modelled)
- retention (being able to recall what you had previously paid attention to)
- reproduction (being able to repeat the action/image/event)
- motivation (is there an incentive to imitate?).

Bandura (1973) postulated that reciprocal determinism was a key factor that influenced the way that someone behaved; that our personality interacts with the environment, the behaviour and our internal worlds.

So what does this mean in terms of relationships? How does this help us understand and recognize the importance of relationships? If we accept that there are a number of factors that influence our behaviours, it then follows that there are a number of factors that influence our relationships. This is not a one-way valve: we can see that relationships also influence behaviour as well as behaviour influencing relationships. From Bandura's (1973) perspective, in order to help and support those around us, and influence behaviour, we need to consider attention, retention, reproduction and motivation.

Some of the aspects discussed above touch upon ideas of behaviour being **learned**, **enforced**, **encouraged** and **normalized**. Learned behaviour refers to behaviours that we emulate after an experience or practice. They do not necessarily have to be embedded or established behaviours (i.e. normalized), and crucially they can be unlearned.

Learned and normalized

> Matthew is 4 years old and is playing in the playground when he hears his friend Livia say 'fart'. Matthew finds this really funny and copies Livia, and says it again when he is in class. Matthew doesn't hear this word at home because his mum and dad call it 'parps'. Matthew's teacher tells him that he shouldn't use that word in school.

This isn't normalized behaviour from Matthew, he is just having fun about a word that he understands is a bit mischievous and silly. He likes his friend Livia and she giggles when she hears her friend say it. If we were to look at Livia we can see that perhaps, while the action is the same, the behaviour is more embedded. In Livia's household the use of the word fart is normalized. She is exposed to this word on a regular basis, and there is no particular negative value placed on the word in her family, unlike Matthew's where an alternative word is used instead. Further to this idea (not to say this happens in Livia's house), if a child is exposed to shouting, swearing and things we may consider disruptive, we may see that these things are normalized in the children we work with. It may be that Livia just uses this word and doesn't realize that others may see it as inappropriate.

Encouraged and enforced

Relationships incorporate how we may experience them through the expectations that are set by others, and this builds into issues around trust and respect. Enforced behaviour is behaviour we feel we have little control over, and can be seen in the context of discipline and punishment. Enforced behaviour is rarely about self-will or any understanding of why the task is being performed. Instead it is linked to the authority of the person attempting to control the outcome. If left to their own devices it is unlikely that the child would behave in this particular way without it being enforced. Enforced behaviours are normally associated with more traditional behavioural management techniques – that punishment for other behaviours will drive behaviours that you want to see next time.

Encouraged behaviour, as the name suggests, is when there is a reinforcement of the behaviours we want to see. This is entwined in relationships that we have with others and perhaps can be characterized by the phrase 'carrot or stick', with the carrot to encourage the donkey to walk rather than enforcement by using the stick to hit the donkey. In encouraged behaviour there may be changes, but this is likely to happen over a longer period of time, and develops from a range of reinforcements, supportive influence from others and (extrinsic or intrinsic) rewards.

How might relationships lead to specific issues in the class?

When you meet a child, whether at early years, primary or secondary school, they will have had a whole range of relationships before the one they may develop with you. A child may have had a typical development of relationships with a relatively unremarkable past. They may have responses to their behaviour (i.e. it was modelled effectively) that mean you would consider the child well-rounded. Below I explore some key areas that we might consider in terms of relationships through a number of vignettes.

Think about a child falling over: what would you expect the reaction from a grown-up be? It may be that the answer to this question depends entirely on the severity of the fall, but I will describe this in more detail.

Validity of emotions

> Ava is 4 years old. She is playing in the playground when another child runs over and tells you that she has fallen over and hurt herself. In walking over to Ava you can see that she has grazed her knee but it doesn't look serious. There are several shallow cuts from some stones from the ground and a little bit of blood.
>
> 'Are you ok Ava?' you ask. Ava bursts into tears and points to her hands which are also grazed from where she tried to break her fall.

It is likely, while being mindful of your own professional boundaries, that you sympathize, give Ava a hug, and say some soothing phrases such as 'there, there, we will clean you up'. In doing this you are essentially validating the child's emotions and their pain. If they have developed secure attachments, the child is likely to respond by slowly stopping their tears and will be reassured by you as an adult. If we extend this to think of more serious events, how does a child learn and know that it is ok to share how they feel? That if they tell you something that is worrying them, they know you will talk through it, and may not give them solutions but help them find their own solutions.

Self-belief

> Robin is 10 years old and has been invited to a friend's birthday party. It is going to be held in a trampoline park that includes a rock climbing wall. Robin has never been rock climbing and says to his dad that he is nervous. His dad says that he understands, but also reminds him that while he has not been rock climbing before, they have gone tree-climbing, and although it's not exactly the same those skills will help him.

Self-belief is the way we feel about ourselves. It can include the way that we judge and characterize what we are good at, how we look, as well as how we behave. If we think about Robin and how his dad has modelled certain characteristics relating to self-belief, his dad responds by validating Robin's emotions (*his dad says that he understands*) but he also promotes resilience and risk-taking. His dad reminds Robin of skills that may be relevant in his next event. Robin's relationship appears to be marked by a consistent approach from his dad: Robin was confident in saying that he was nervous, and his dad responded by validating his emotions before providing encouragement. This in turn is likely to support Robin in trying new things and being able to understand that he can generalize his skills across different activities. Looking back to Bandura (1973) and concepts around motivation, we can see that the motivation for this event will reaffirm the risk-taking of trying something new. The party is likely to be fun and enjoyable for Robin, therefore meaning the risk-taking event of rock climbing is valued and he then further develops a confident sense of self.

Resolution

> Jaspreet is in the car with her mum when another car knocks the wing mirror off their car. Her mum is annoyed and says that the wing mirror is expensive to replace. Jaspreet sits in the car and listens to her mum talking to the other driver. Her mum acknowledges that she was driving too high up the road and it was her fault that the wing mirror has come off. Both drivers inspect the damage and the

Recognizing relationships

> conversation ends with Jaspreet's mum and the other driver agreeing that they won't worry about going through insurance as that will cost more on premiums. Instead they swap numbers and Jaspreet's mum will arrange for her own wing mirror to be fixed and pay for the slight damage on the other person's car.

In this case study there could have been a number of alternative outcomes. There could have been swearing and shouting, and general frustration shown by both parties. Instead what is modelled to Jaspreet is that while things that are annoying and difficult may happen, they can be resolved amicably. This is a good foundation for Jaspreet, who is learning from this modelling that it is ok to say sorry rather than avoiding what happened, and there are ways of rectifying situations other than verbal aggression.

Focus

> On a Friday night Andres brings homework back from school. His mum and dad tell him that he isn't to play computer games until he has completed his work. Andres does his homework at the kitchen table while his dad cooks dinner. There are some questions that Andres finds a bit more difficult but his dad interrupts the cooking and sits down next to him to just give him a bit of guidance before carrying on with the food. 'I remember doing this at school', his dad says fondly while carrying on stirring the sauce for the pasta.

In this vignette we hear about Andres and his dad helping him with his homework. Andres has a particular space in which to do his homework, and while not in a distraction-free environment the relationship here is key. It is clear from his dad's approach that there is a high value placed on education. This perspective on education is likely to support Andres in developing a whole range of positive behaviours, but moreover the way that his dad talks fondly about it affects his and his son's relationship.

Trust

> Wassim is learning how to swim and his mum is in the swimming pool with him. Wassim doesn't want to get in the swimming pool and tells her this. You don't need to worry, she tells him, it is only this deep, and shows him that the water will only come up to his chest. Wassim tentatively approaches the water and she holds his hand. The water is as his mum says, and just reaches his chest. His mum continues to explain some of the signs in the water and shows him clearly where she won't be able to reach the floor.

In trusting someone there is a sense that you can see that others are reliable, and for a child this is heavily tied into secure attachments and knowing that the person looking after you holds you in mind and can be relied upon to keep you safe. Developing relationships that are based on mutual trust and respect can be a firm way of providing the foundations for positive relationships in school and beyond the school gate. Wassim's mum in the vignette tells him the truth; she is clear about where the pool is shallow and where it is deep. Wassim is learning that his mum is trustworthy, helping him build his confidence in a core skill, while appreciating that he is worried about swimming.

Behaviour is influenced by the key relationships that we have in our lives. When we look at trying to understand behaviour, a central tenet is that relationships are another way of trying to unpick and understand the things that are happening in our class.

References

Bandura, A. (1973) *Aggression: A Social Learning Analysis*. Englewood Cliffs, NJ: Prentice-Hall.

Nurture UK *What is nurture?* Available at: https://www.nurtureuk.org/nurture/what-nurture (accessed 23 August 2020).

Ofsted (2011) *Supporting Children with Challenging Behaviour through a Nurture Group Approach*, Ofsted website. Available at: https://www.gov.uk/government/publications/supporting-children-with-challenging-behaviour (accessed 1 November 2020).

Part

Responding

Part III

Responding

10 Individual preparation

Debates on how we manage behaviour are rife and conflicting, and what is considered the best approach is contested. There are a plethora of approaches that look at ways of changing the behaviour of children, but fewer on how to support children's emotional health. An example of how to change the behaviour of children is included in Bennett's (2017) work on how school leaders can develop a school culture to encourage positive behaviours. With ideas around the need to reinforce the norms and values of the schooling environment, Bennett considers 'social norms' as a central, driving part of school culture:

> Social norms are found most clearly in the routines of the school. Any aspect of school behaviour that can be standardized because it is expected from all students at all times should be, for example walking on the left or right of the corridor, entering the class, entering assembly, clearing tables at lunch. (Bennett, 2017: 31)

There is less focus on individual needs but more on how schools can reiterate their school culture in shaping the behaviour of children. This often leads to oversimplified and polarized debates, where we may see those that recommend trauma-informed approaches and nurture standing in opposition to advocates of what are sometimes seen as more traditionalist approaches. However, the reality is that each child needs to be responded to differently, and while some may provide a formula to work through some of the issues (as in the five-stage formula that underpins the parts of this handbook), it would be impossible to provide guidance on every circumstance that you may face in your professional career. Instead the reality is that just as children will exhibit different behaviours there will be a range of underlying reasons, various interplays between systems and personal histories, that may go to drive some aspects of their behaviour.

This is where the fundamental issue arises with behavioural management, that there is an assumption that quick-fix solutions represented by simple dichotomies and implemented in the classroom will be the ultimate solution. In these polarized approaches we also see that the hope that certain approaches using punishment for infraction of rules will rectify the issue. Instead, resorting to isolation rooms or segregated booths only serves to further isolate an individual, and this is unlikely to support a child in developing further strategies or alternatives to behaviour that makes it more challenging for the teacher to teach. We also know that fixed-term and permanent exclusions still exist, with significant concerns that a high proportion of adults who appear in our criminal justice system have had a history of exclusions. The Forgotten Children report (Home Office, 2018) references several children's journeys towards exclusion and the current behavioural systems that failed them and only fostered further experiences of not belonging:

> Many of the young people we spoke to talked about being put in isolation in mainstream school for large parts of academic years. Some of the pupils were put in isolation for behavioural reasons, while others were removed from the classroom for other reasons, including because they were victims of bullying. The young people told us about the impact that isolation had on them. One young person who was isolated because they had been bullied told us that 'With that kind of support, I gave up with the school system—I chose not to go'. (Home Office, 2018: 26)

In addition to the myriad concerns expressed in the Forgotten Children report, we know that one of the biggest risk factors for children isn't whether or not they behave badly, but whether or not they will kill themselves. Suicide is the leading cause of death in children and yet our focus is on reactive and often punitive approaches. If punishment isn't working, then how do we implement and respond, from an individual perspective, about how we support rather than punish? How do we influence rather than control?

We must begin individually and from the position that every child matters, and every child deserves to make mistakes as well as have a chance – that all children are entitled to embrace an enriching and engaging education.

Understanding the causes and reasons behind unwanted behaviour can provide a helpful framework in order to individually respond to those behaviours which we deem unhelpful. In previous chapters I have focused on a range of children's stories and considered ideas about how to notice, identify and understand their needs.

In this chapter, I look specifically at one child whose behaviour may be referred to as 'challenging'. These are the typical behaviours that may be cited when a child is excluded from school for 'persistent disruptive behaviour', and ones which make it really difficult for a teacher to focus on the lesson and its content. To illustrate, I am going to use the case of Benjamin to help us think of how we might plan an approach and consider resources.

> Benjamin is a white British boy who is 14 years of age. He has had several fixed-term exclusions for his behaviour, which includes swearing at staff, walking out of lessons, refusing to follow instructions such as to retrieve his book from the back of the class and regularly pushing in the dinner queue past the younger students. Benjamin has a group of friends that he hangs around with after school and they play football in the park. He has never openly said so but you suspect that he smokes cannabis and has had his bag searched a number of times after a distinctive smell was reported to come from his bag.
>
> Benjamin is generally dishevelled when he comes into school, which is invariably late although he doesn't live that far away. He enjoys physical education

> (PE) and especially football, and stays after school to play in the football club. Benjamin comes from a single parent family and his mum has recently met a new partner, but Benjamin sees his dad regularly and helps him in his workshop at the weekends as a panel beater. Benjamin is a confident reader and you have heard from your colleagues that he will happily engage in debates in subjects such as history. You teach him three times a week for maths, and you dread his lessons. He talks over you, argues about sitting in his seat and is generally uncooperative. You also find him physically threatening: he is tall, and will often step nearer to you than you feel comfortable with. He has never been physically aggressive in school but he will often exit the class loudly.

We will return to Benjamin and his story as we explore ideas around our individual responses. Teaching is not just about the curriculum, the lesson material and pedagogy. Perhaps it should be, but that may be a discussion for a different book! Teaching invariably includes the relationships we have: with our students, our colleagues and the wider school community. These all have an effect on how we may individually prepare for some of the challenges we are likely to encounter in the classroom environment. While this chapter focuses on individual preparation, it should also be considered in the wider context, in the later chapters covering structural preparation and execution, to consider the wider school culture.

The first aspect to consider in relation to individual preparation is our own vulnerabilities. We all come into teaching with our own histories, our own stories, beliefs and understanding of the world. With that we may become frustrated, angry or annoyed by something that perhaps a colleague would not be. I start with the assumption that as teachers, we want to go into the classroom and teach in a way that is interesting and engaging and imparts knowledge. When this is thwarted by the actions of others it can be incredibly difficult to demonstrate our frustrations and angers in the classroom. While wider parliamentary reviews are more clear about the structural changes that need to be put in place (Timpson, 2019; Forgotten Children, 2018), there is less consideration of individual preparation to help develop a classroom culture that supports positive behaviour of children with a range of needs.

This is possibly a controversial aspect, but a response goes back to before we even begin to notice behaviours. It is when we think about the curriculum we deliver, the way we plan lessons and think about the children in our classes.

In earlier chapters, I set out the issues that we may notice with children who have a range of needs (see Chapter 2 on identification in particular). If we do not plan lessons which are accessible for children, which set out our expectations and reiterate the values that we feel are important in the class, then, while this is still unacceptable, we may notice that children don't behave in ways that are conducive for learning. It is important that children, especially those that struggle more, have a clear sense of what is next in the class. Below I have broken down some aspects of Benjamin's story to help move through the five stages of understanding.

To notice

What you have heard:

1 Benjamin enjoys reading out loud.
2 Benjamin will engage in verbal discussions in history.
3 Benjamin seems to enjoy spending time with his dad at the weekends.

What you have noticed:

1 Benjamin arrives late to school.
2 Benjamin does not appear clean.
3 Benjamin does little work in maths.
4 Benjamin argues about sitting in a specific seat in a lesson.

To understand

Accessing Benjamin's internal world may be very difficult. You will notice that the case study demonstrates a poor relationship with the maths teacher in this instance (it could easily be the English teacher, the PE teacher, etc., depending on the individual child and your own specialism). Here, we are looking at preparing an individual to respond, and move beyond the cycle of arguments and debates. One thing that may be helpful is to observe another teacher's class. That isn't to say they teach better, but they may employ different strategies that could be helpful. Use the following to prompt questions and develop understanding:

1 How does the teacher greet Benjamin when he comes into the classroom?
2 Where does Benjamin sit?
3 Are there phases of the lessons or transitions, and how are these managed by the teacher?
4 Are there physical differences between myself and the teacher (i.e. gender) that for whatever reason may make Benjamin feel more confident, safer or even more worried?
5 Are there different opportunities relating to groupwork?
6 Are the same rules being employed in the classroom across the school?
7 Does the teacher or support staff provide alternative strategies for engagement (now and next cards, visual prompts, quiet direction once the class is on task)?

The purpose of asking these questions is to prompt your own individual preparation. In trying to figure out the answers to these questions we are looking at ways to minimize the need to move on to the next stages of individual execution and how we can respond effectively. Much of our own individual preparation comes from asking questions of ourselves to try to explore the wider structural issues that we may be re-enacting in our classroom and our own behaviours.

References

Bennett, T. (2017) *Creating a Culture: How School Leaders Can Optimise Behaviour*. London: Department for Education.

Burstow, P., Newbigging, K., Tew, J. and Costello, B. (2018) *Investing in a Resilient Generation: Keys to a Mentally Prosperous Nation*. Birmingham: University of Birmingham.

Home Office (2018) *Forgotten Children: Alternative Provision and the Scandal of Ever Increasing Exclusions*. London: Home Office. Available at: https://publications.parliament.uk/pa/cm201719/cmselect/cmeduc/342/342.pdf (accessed 1 November 2020).

Papyrus: Prevention of young suicide. Available at: https://papyrus-uk.org/ (accessed 5 June 2020).

Timpson, E. (2019) *Timpson Review of School Exclusion*. London: DfE.

11 Responding: individual execution

When we were looking at how to identify behaviours, we explored the use of Phoenix Frameworks. These frameworks are designed to help us provide a more nuanced description, and therefore a much better understanding of the behaviours children present in the classroom and beyond.

When it comes to responding to individual pupils in your classroom, you can once again refer to the Phoenix Frameworks to help you understand how you can best support them.

It is important to note that Phoenix Frameworks are not medically approved and are not designed to create diagnoses. However, they should signpost you to appropriate and effective solutions and initiatives for the provision of support and assistance.

In this chapter we will revisit the frameworks we explored in the Identifying part of the book, and explore what our nuanced description and targeted understanding of behaviour means when it comes to responding.

Anger

By understanding the direction of anger and an individual's ability to control it, the framework that looks at anger creates the following four quadrants.

Direct and planned

Anger in this quadrant will be specific (anger at an individual pupil or teacher) and will show elements of planning and preparation. In this position it is useful to initially explore the reason for the anger. It is likely that your pupil will have a reason for both the target of their anger and the actions they have taken, and it is ok to agree with that reasoning. There are many things in life that may make us angry but what's important when it comes to our behaviour is being able to manage and control it appropriately. Essentially, anger is ok to feel and express but not in ways that hurt or damage other people.

To that end, it will be useful to look at the child's understanding of boundaries, appropriate behaviours, morality and guidance. It can be useful to ask them to justify their actions – do they think it is acceptable? This in turn should help you further explore all influences, normalized thoughts/actions, as well as

Figure 11.1 Responding to anger

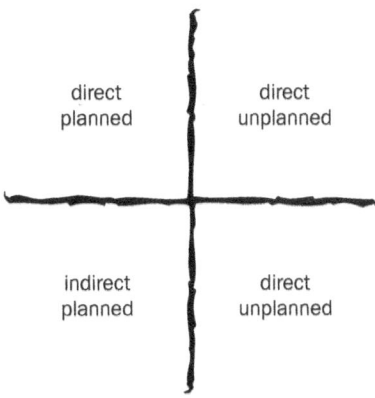

influences in their home environment. As a precaution, it is beneficial to look at any historical behavioural issues to ensure the pupil's anger isn't hiding underlying mental health issues or may relate to events that may require safeguarding input and support.

Direct and unexpected

An unexpected but targeted outburst of anger is something that needs to be explored gently. It is likely that an individual behaving in this manner has displayed some form of trauma response, and initially you should ensure your pupil is in a safe environment where they feel supported before you begin to respond. Engage with them to examine the trigger or tipping point that led to the outburst of anger. Explore the emotions that underpin this; is there trauma, neglect or abuse that is happening either in school or at home? Are there historic events that are causing emotional challenges or mental health issues? It's important to note the directive nature of the anger and try to understand if there was transference at play, a need for control, or if the target presented a safe (for them) opportunity for your pupil to express their emotions. If a trauma response is detected or confirmed, it will be useful to give your pupil alternative ways of expressing their anger and safe environments for them to do so in context to their age and understanding.

Indirect and planned

A pupil who has expressed anger in this way is likely to have used their anger to not only communicate their feelings but also draw attention to them. A planned angry outburst indicates that this pupil wants you and others to know they are angry, and this might be done to fuel a need for control or attention. This may be an ongoing and repetitive need, in which case it may be that this pupil doesn't receive any control or attention at home, or it may be their way of asking for help, reaching out and sharing some of the things they are feeling.

Indirect and unexpected

In this position, your pupil is likely to have experienced an uncontrollable outburst of anger. This is likely to have been a traumatic experience for them, they may feel emotional and exhausted, and it is recommended that you comfort rather than confront them. Your pupil probably has challenges with emotional regulation and this is often a neurological imprint caused by early childhood trauma. The prefrontal cortex (the front of our brain) is the hub of emotional management and impulse control. When we experience extreme trauma in our early years, the development of the prefrontal cortex is hindered, making it much harder for individuals to control their emotions during childhood and into adulthood. If your pupil is able to identify any source of trauma or abuse in their childhood, they are likely to need some professional support in the management of this, and as their teacher you should focus on helping them feel safe and confident that they will be cared for and will be able to find a solution in the future.

Withdrawal

By understanding the reason a pupil seems to be withdrawn and how consistently their withdrawn behaviour occurs, we are able to create the four outcomes below.

Figure 11.2 Responding to withdrawal

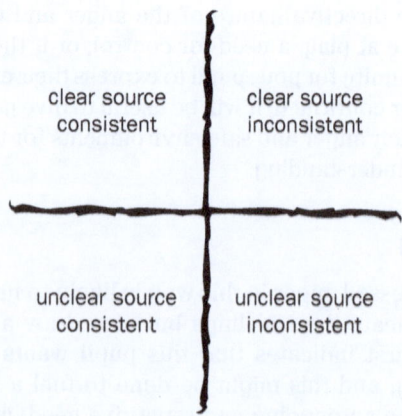

Clear source and consistent

Although your pupil is likely to often seem withdrawn, being able to understand the reason for this is beneficial and goes some way to making an effective solution possible. With your pupil, you should explore their emotions, previous experiences and current perception of the source. You can creatively explore different settings, environments or opportunities that may change their perception or understanding of the source of their withdrawal – or their response to it. In this position, you can use some simple score cards and scenario testing to see what would make your pupil's need to withdraw higher or lower, and present some reasonable adjustment that could be used to support them while they are in class.

Clear source and inconsistent

If your pupil has a clear reason for their withdrawal but they don't always feel they have to act on it, it's important to understand what interactions lead to them withdrawing, and what differences mean they are able to remain engaged. Work with your pupil to explore and really understand what happens when they feel uncomfortable but are able to remain engaged. What is the reasoning, thinking or coping mechanisms that they use and how can you work together to increase their access to these resources?

Unclear source and consistent

If your pupil is consistently withdrawn but unable to explain why, it is likely that there are internal causes for their behaviour. Initially, it is important to ask if they are comfortable with withdrawing. If it is simply part of their personality, and a part they are happy with, then there is no need for us to challenge, question or support it. You may like to highlight what they may miss by withdrawing or what they may gain if they engage, but fundamentally, if your pupil's behaviour doesn't trouble them, forcing interaction and engagement is unlikely to be beneficial. However, if your pupil is uncomfortable with their withdrawal and feels this is something they would like to change, then you should begin gently exploring their confidence, self-esteem and self-worth. Ask your pupil if there is anything that they believe would help them with their emotions, rather than specifically with their withdrawn behaviour. Are there ways that they would prefer to communicate or any changes that could be made to their environment to make them feel more supported, comfortable or confident?

Unclear source and inconsistent

When your pupil is in this position, the first useful thing to do is to keep a diary to help identify and understand possible triggers or causes of their withdrawn behaviour. It's important to explore a variety of triggers including hormones, diet, sleep routines and more typical contributors such as trauma, abuse and neglect.

Work with your pupil to explore their home environment, their understanding of social norms and the nature of the key relationships they have. Try to identify inconsistencies in your pupil's life that could be the cause of their withdrawal.

Insecurity

By identifying when your pupil may feel insecure and the impact this has on their behaviours, we are able to create the four outcomes below.

Figure 11.3 Responding to insecurity

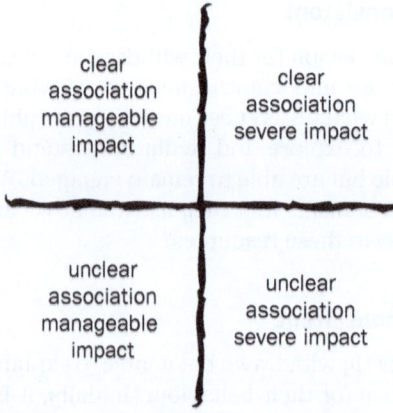

Clear association and severe impact

Insecurity of this nature is likely to be a result of situational-specific anxiety and may indicate some form of abuse, whether that's bullying at school or issues at home. This type of insecurity could also be indicative of historic trauma or some form of post-traumatic stress disorder. It can be useful to explore emotions like guilt and engage in tasks that explore and develop your pupil's understanding and sense of self-worth and self-esteem. With a clear association, it can be incredibly useful to explore the situations in which your pupil doesn't feel insecure and is able to experience some sense of confidence. Understand these situations and see if there are any opportunities to reframe, recreate or transfer these experiences and more positive thought patterns to the situations in which your pupil feels most insecure.

Clear association and manageable impact

This position indicates that there are some things in your pupil's life that make them feel uncomfortable, but a manageable impact suggests that they have a good sense of awareness and strong coping mechanisms. It is important to work with your pupil to develop and strengthen the self-protecting methods they currently use and ensure they are given appropriate resources and the support they need to execute them. You should be asking your pupil how you can make managing the impact easier for them and how you can reduce their exposure to the things that make them feel most insecure in their learning environment.

Unclear association and severe impact

The combination of factors in this position suggest that the pupil may be experiencing maladaptive thinking, which could be a strong indicator of underlying mental health issues. Pupils in this position may also be at significant risk of self-harm or suicidal tendencies, so you need to monitor them closely and ensure they receive a medical assessment urgently. It is important to ask your pupil if they feel safe at school, if they feel safe at home and if there is anything they can think of that could improve the way they are feeling.

Unclear association and manageable impact

In this position, you should be working with your pupil to understand how they manage the insecurities they are experiencing. Use various methods to understand their thought processes, their coping mechanisms and the environments in which they find their insecurity is at its worst. Ensure your pupil recognizes that it is perfectly normal to feel confident in some circumstances and insecure in others. There are some situations in which we feel very comfortable and others that make us feel incredibly nervous, and these are 'normal', healthy responses to new or challenging situations. It can be useful to keep a confidence diary so that you and your pupil are able to monitor if their insecurity is problematic or a part of everyday emotional responses.

Intolerance – understanding/enforcement

By recognizing an individual's understanding of their intolerances and their ability to control how and when they act on them, we are able to create the four options for responding below.

Good understanding and enforced

In this position, your pupil is doing really well to understand their intolerance but struggling to manage how they respond to their emotions. You should work with your pupil to use the understanding that they are able to demonstrate and challenge the script that surrounds it. It is possible that they have taken one rule or one stereotype and applied it to many situations, circumstances or

Figure 11.4 Responding to intolerance

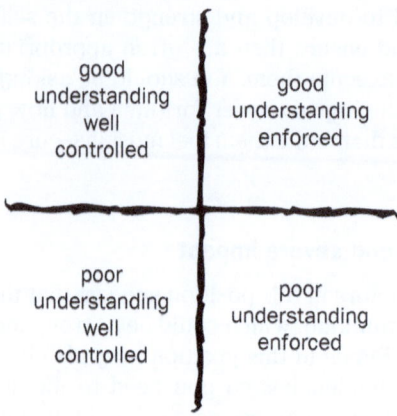

individuals. It is useful to explore whether unconscious bias may be at play and use storytelling that challenges stereotypes of widely applied opinions. You can work with your pupil to explore whether they believe their response is rational or inflated, or if they are able to identify where their intolerance came from.

Good understanding and controlled

In this position, your pupil is doing really well to manage their intolerance and it is important that you praise them for this. It is your role to understand the long-term viability of their control mechanisms and assess any impact this could have on their long-term physical and mental health. You can explore how transferable their understanding and coping mechanisms are to other circumstances, and how long they have held the existing intolerances, to see if understanding this gives you and your pupil the opportunity to work together to resolve or evolve the thinking that surrounds them.

Poor understanding and enforced

This combination of factors suggests that there may be some unresolved trauma or ongoing abuse that is leading to a need for control or resistance. You can explore triggers with your pupil and look for indicators of historic or current trauma and abuse. Understanding the script that leads to intolerance provides us with a framework for understanding where some of the emotions come from and what feelings accompany or fuel your pupil's intolerance. These feelings may include need for control, jealousy, justice, guilt, greed or opportunity. It is important that, rather than punishing or restricting your pupil's ability to enforce their intolerance, you work instead to understand the reasons behind it and support your pupil to resolve those reasons, and in turn improve their behaviour and ability to control their intolerance.

Poor understanding and controlled

Controlling or regulating something you don't understand is likely to be a drain on your cognitive resources and ultimately will make controlling intolerances challenging in the long term. It is likely to make your pupil cognitively inefficient in other areas and may impact on their ability to concentrate, focus and or interact with others. Help your pupil understand the source of their intolerance by exploring areas of resistance. Encourage them to put a measure to their feelings of intolerance and keep note of them in a diary which, when reflected upon, should help them better understand what creates their sense of intolerance and when.

Apathy

By identifying a pupil's level of empathy and their ability to interact with others, we are able to create the four positions and appropriate responding recommendations that follow.

Figure 11.5 Responding to apathy

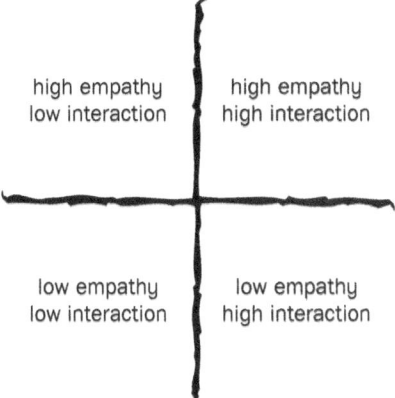

High empathy and high interaction

If your pupil is presenting apathetic behaviour but shows high levels of empathy and frequent, effective interaction, it may suggest that they are simply bored, disengaged or otherwise disinterested in the subject matter that is being presented at school. You may wish to explore the age-appropriateness of the topics you are covering and how the pupil regards work in terms of interest and difficulty. With high levels of interaction you should be able to explore and ultimately understand the reason for their lack of interest and engagement, and work with them to overcome this. It can be worth thinking about whether your pupil is looking for praise, reward or recognition or if they need alternative forms of stimulation.

High empathy and low interaction

In this position, it is likely that your pupil is experiencing some kind of anxiety around a specific task or interaction. This relationship of factors indicates that your pupil may have a problem with expressing feelings and emotions rather than having or recognizing them in the first place. It is possible, and common, for children in this position to feel that they aren't able to trust anyone with their feelings. They may have been mocked or mimicked in the past for voicing concerns or worries, and have then chosen to keep their feelings internalized. Help your pupil explore their feelings and emotions by providing them with a safe space, various forms of communication and a commitment of understanding and support.

Low empathy and high interaction

This combination of high interaction and low empathy may make your pupil behave in ways that may be considered socially inappropriate. It could indicate an underlying cognitive condition such as Asperger's syndrome or autistic spectrum condition. If your pupil shows little understanding of social appropriateness, personal boundaries and appropriate behaviour, you should initially begin the CYPMHS referral process. You can make the referral robust and useful by exploring underlying issues relating to defiance and attention seeking, and you can use additional frameworks from this book to explore those areas effectively. Work with your pupil to see if they are intentionally flouting social boundaries or simply don't understand them. If your pupil seems to be choosing to show little empathy towards others, you should again make a referral to CYPMHS and explore whether there may be current or historic abuse or trauma. Low empathy tends to be shown by children and young people that have experienced horrific, prolonged abuse from significant adults or primary caregivers, and in this instance it is likely to be used as a survival mechanism.

Low empathy and low interaction

This is a very difficult position for your pupil to be in – and a challenging position for you to respond to. It is likely that low empathy combined with low interaction will be indicative of either cognitive challenges or disorders or it may mask extreme trauma. As a starting point, you would try to explore emotions using non-invasive forms of communication like arts, crafts and imaginary play. Your primary focus will be to establish a sense of trust and develop interaction in a way that makes your pupil feel safe and will allow you to develop an understanding of their circumstances by using cue cards, word association and memory tasks.

Defiance

By exploring the purpose of a pupil's defiance and the ways in which this behaviour is connected to their identity, we are able to understand more and respond in one of the four ways detailed below.

Figure 11.6 Responding to defiance

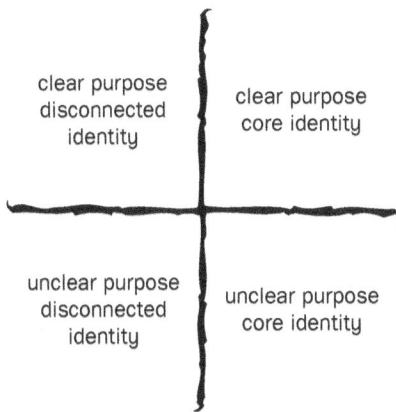

Clear purpose and core identity

In this position, it is likely that your pupil will be gaining some sense of identity and belonging from being part of a gang, club or group that shows defiance against certain things or specific people. To help support them, it is important to initially understand why they don't otherwise have a sense of belonging and what has prevented them from experiencing this in more traditional forms (family unit, peer groups, etc.). A sense of belonging is crucial to human survival and it is beneficial to explore this notion with your pupil. You can complete a number of tasks that look at alternative sources of belonging and ask your pupil to appraise each one with regard to how they will affect them in both the short and the long term. Help your pupil to acknowledge the short- and long-term implications of their behaviour and present alternative outcomes for their future, their relationships and their engagement in society if they can change their values and purpose with regard to defiance at this stage. It is also useful to work with your pupil to help them find less defiant ways of fulfilling their purpose or passion without jeopardizing their identity, behaviour or opportunities in the future.

Clear purpose and disconnected identity

In this position the defiance your pupil presents is likely to be an interest, a passion or an individual commitment that shapes part of their current interests but isn't intrinsically linked to their identity. Your pupil could be showing defiance against animal testing, for example, because it is currently 'on trend' to do so. They might be misbehaving because they have realized it is 'cool' to do so, but unlike in other positions, the driver for their behaviour is likely to be social acceptance rather than a real passion, belief or commitment to the cause. It's worth noting that as children become adults, having interests or passions is incredibly healthy and some people will show defiance in various aspects of their life, simply as a part of their personality. It is only if this behaviour is distressing to the pupil or incredibly disruptive to your classroom that it needs to be challenged. Providing alternative ways of meeting their purpose is most likely to be useful at this stage and shouldn't be met with too much resistance given that it isn't part of the pupil's identity.

Unclear purpose and core identity

Although the reasons for your pupil's defiance are unclear, in this position it is likely to be due to one of two things. If the pupil is defiant along with others (in a group or gang, for example) it is likely that they have a need for a sense of belonging and they find this by being defiant with similar pupils. In this instance, it is important to explore why a sense of belonging is absent from this pupil's life and gently try to understand why they are having to get a sense of community and acceptance through negative group association. If your pupil is defiant alone, their behaviour is likely to be a form of self-sabotage, rejection or fear of acceptance that will be fuelled by insecurity or trauma response. In these circumstances, ensure you speak to them in a safe and welcoming environment. Be gentle in your body language and supportive in your tone of voice. It is always useful to begin by asking them what they understand about defiance, what they believe the short- and long-term outcomes will be and if they can identify or describe alternative behaviours that will be less disruptive but as effective in sharing their concerns, needs or problems. Assure them that their voice will be heard and opinions respected, but suggest other ways of communicating their needs. Explore where and how else they demonstrate defiance to check whether this is a universal or school-specific behaviour.

Unclear purpose and disconnected identity

Pupils in this position are likely to be practising their need for control or desire to have their voice heard. This need may be more dramatic due to trauma, abuse, underlying mental health conditions or a variety of insecurities and challenges that drive the pupil to defy rules and authority. In the first instance, the most valuable thing to do with this pupil is establish a sense of trust. Help your pupil feel comfortable, showcase some of your own weaknesses or vulnerabilities and explore different forms of communication that can be utilized inside and outside of the classroom. It will be useful to provide positive examples of how and where other pupils have been able to establish a sense of belonging, explore independent interests and have their voices heard in ways that aren't defiant but are very powerful.

Sadness

By identifying how much your pupil understands why they are sad, and reflecting on their own emotional insight, we are able to explore sadness in more detail using the outcomes below.

Figure 11.7 Responding to sadness

Good understanding and strong insight

In this position, it is likely that your pupil has experienced some traumatic events or is experiencing ongoing trauma. This understood and acknowledged sadness may also be the result of a combination of stressors which you should look to list and analyse with the child as part of the process of support. Although your pupil feels sad at the moment, their insight and understanding of this minimizes the concern of severe mental illness and gives you information around how to best help and support their mood. Some useful exploratory questions may include: How long have you felt sad? How often do you feel sad? What helps you feel less sad? Can you draw a picture of your sadness? Can you write a letter to your sadness? Make a list of the things that make you feel less sad. What would you need to feel happy more often? It is essential that even though sadness is a common emotion for many of us, you ensure that your own emotional world does not adversely affect your pupil.

Good understanding and weak insight

In this position it is likely that your pupil understands why they should feel sad, but they feel very disconnected from their emotions. This survival mechanism often occurs in response to traumatic experiences, and can indicate more problematic mental health issues. Dissociation can be incredibly damaging so if you see this present in your pupil's behaviours, it will be useful to make a CYPMHS referral so that they are able to explore this further. In this situation there is a risk associated with exploring emotions and their causes in too much detail and, as a teacher, it is ill-advised for you to begin exploring trauma that you may not be able to efficiently respond to. Ensure your pupil knows that you are there for them, that you want them to be happy, that they deserve to be happy and that you will work with them to provide support, care and guidance wherever possible.

Poor understanding and strong insight

In this position, it is recommended to initially explore whether your pupil's poor understanding of their emotions is due to an inability to understand or a lack of knowledge. Give them the opportunity to understand things that might make them feel sad – look at instances in which others are sad and use storytelling to measure your pupil's response to sadness and other people's reasons for it in different parts of society. Work to slowly expand on the themes they seem to engage with or relate to most, and talk about the characters and circumstances you present. Use your pupil's strong insight and ask them to explain their sadness. Encourage them to describe what it feels like, when it is with them and when it is worse. Which book character does their sadness remind them of? What food would their sadness be? Ask lots of unusual questions to encourage conversation and exploration.

If there is a continued lack of understanding around sadness and no clear reason for your pupil to be feeling this way, you should refer them to their GP in the first instance, to explore the possibility of depression and other mood disorders.

Poor understanding and weak insight

In this position, there are a number of possibilities relating to the sadness your pupil is expressing and your first job is to work to decipher which of these are most likely to be making your pupil feel sad. In the most simplistic terms, your pupil might be copying behaviour that they have seen in others. It is important to ask which emotions they do understand, and where and when they may have seen other people display sadness. You can ask some simple questions around other people expressing their feelings, for example: How often do they see people cry? How often do they hear people laugh? What does being sad mean for them? Do they know anyone else who feels sad often? Help your pupil explore their own emotions by providing outlines of bodies, faces, brains. Ask them to fill each outline with words that describe their feelings or drawings/doodles that show how they feel. You can use tasks like this, along with a mood diary, to closely monitor your pupil's mood. It is also useful to ensure they are surrounded by support. Use storytelling, and explore providing a buddy who has experienced or overcome trauma or mental health problems.

Attention seeking

By identifying the nature and persistence of your pupil's attention seeking, you will be able to respond in one of the following four ways.

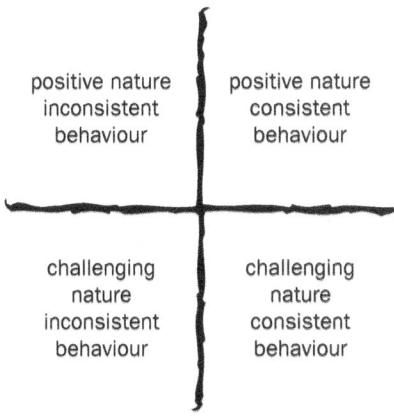

Figure 11.8 Responding to attention seeking

Positive and consistent

Although positive behaviour is often less disruptive than negative attention seeking, a constant need for attention indicates an underlying need that isn't being met. A pupil in this position is also at risk of becoming more disruptive and negative in their attention seeking if these needs are not fulfilled. It's important to explore your pupil's self-esteem, insecurities and understanding of their need for praise and reinforcement. Explore where and how they get this reinforcement when they are not in the classroom, and understand when and how they get praise and attention at home. There are many factors that could influence this, like how many siblings they have, how much their parents work and how often they are at home. You can establish the nature of your pupil's relationship with their parents by asking them what their parents think they are good at, what their parents might say about them today, what their parents said about their last school report, etc. With a pupil in this position, you can implement a reward system that they can use while ensuring they have a structured and controlled opportunity for praise, reward and recognition on a one-to-one basis.

Positive and inconsistent

In this position, you should look to explore the underlying need this behaviour indicates. It suggests that there may be some inconsistent issues at home or in the classroom that make your pupil feel insecure, needy or otherwise in need of praise. It may be the behavioural needs of siblings, challenges within their wider family unit or interactions with other pupils. Or it could be down to the subjects you are covering or the style of learning used at any given time. In some cases there may be forms of emotional abuse or this behaviour could indicate an insecure attachment style or reactive attachment disorder. Although positive attention seeking may not seem overwhelmingly disruptive or challenging, it is important to bear in mind that if this need is not met then it can easily turn into negative, disruptive behaviour that has greater adverse impacts. Help your pupil understand by creating a mood diary and a reward chart – allow them to easily indicate when they need more support, reinforcement or reassurance and explore ways they can boost their sense of belonging and esteem with groups, clubs and extracurricular activities.

Challenging and consistent

It is important to understand that all forms of attention seeking indicate a similar need – whether it is negative or positive attention. It is likely that children who are consistently challenging and disruptive are looking for reinforcement, engagement and support due to insecurity, low self-esteem or parental neglect. Although it is often easy to punish challenging behaviour and control it with restrictions and isolations, it's important to recognize that these pupils are asking for help, crying for attention and obviously not getting it elsewhere. Help your pupil feel heard, safe and respected. Ensure they feel that they have your attention and support, and show kindness in exploring their circumstances at home and the nature of their key relationships. Help your pupil understand that they will be able to get your attention in more positive ways and help them explore how they can establish and improve their self-esteem and confidence. In this position, it can also be useful to allow your pupil to define how they would like to be rewarded – work with them to think about which type of recognition or reward is most meaningful to them, and use this wherever possible.

Challenging and inconsistent

The inconsistent but challenging nature of this attention seeking may indicate an underlying mood disorder, trauma response or attachment disorder. It may suggest there are problems at home or in the classroom that sometimes create a need for attention. It is useful to try to determine what factors make your pupil feel they need additional attention or support, and to discuss with them more appropriate and less disruptive ways of seeking attention and gaining reassurance from people around them. You may be able to explore with your pupil other ways they can have their emotional needs met or different forms of support or attention that will be less disruptive and detrimental. It is critical that, even though the child is presenting challenging behaviours, we don't minimize their need for support, guidance and reassurance. This need should be addressed and attended to before the challenging or disruptive behaviours themselves are explored. Rather than punishing your pupil for this behaviour, it can be useful to try other responses; you can explain the difficulties their behaviours create for you as a teacher and make a deal or agreement that allows you and your pupil to work together to support their needs and rectify their challenging behaviours.

Violence

By understanding the severity of the violence and the ways in which it is reinforced in any pupil's life, you can understand and respond using one of the four positions below.

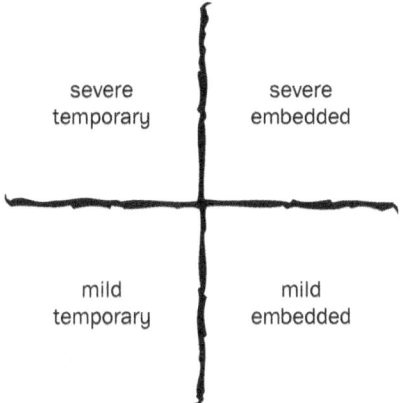

Figure 11.9 Responding to violence

Severe and embedded

This is a challenging position to be in and it suggests that being incredibly violent is part of your pupil's identity. It is likely that they are part of a gang and regularly practise violence and serious crime. It is vital to try to understand if your pupil has a historic experience of violence and abuse in their family life. It is also useful to explore their sense of belonging and understand where they are able to establish their identity, sense of community and social spirit. You can use the other frameworks in this book to explore indicators of mental health issues, think about attachment styles and understand historic trauma, abuse and neglect. It can help to involve additional agencies such as social services and consider introducing an Education, Health and Care Plan (EHCP) to support any additional needs the child has. Think about any reasonable adjustments you can make to support your pupil and understand how they might be able to best control their mood and limit harm or disruption to other children. It is absolutely vital in this position that you are able to complete a risk assessment to determine whether this pupil is 'safe at school' or if they present a significant risk of harm to themselves or others.

Mild and embedded

Being violent towards objects and aggressive in nature is in many cases the thin end of a wedge and it can easily escalate to more severe incidents of violence, particularly when violence has become a part of an individual's identity. It's important to review the other factors in this chapter to understand what needs this child might be fulfilling through their demonstration of violence. Explore where they have an established sense of belonging, what behaviours they might have learned and if there are any cases of abuse, violence or neglect in their history or current background. Give them a safe environment to explore emotions, and confirm that they have your attention and that their opinions will be respected. Consider introducing your pupil to rehabilitated young offenders or use storytelling to help them understand the effects of their actions and the potential impact they could have on their future. Explore their hopes and ambitions – what would they like to be known for? Encourage them to write a letter to their future self and one to their parents (or other significant caregivers) from a troubled future.

Severe and temporary

If your pupil is showing severe violence but it is temporary and out of character, it is essential to try to understand both what has caused them to feel so angry and what has caused them to respond with violence. A demonstration of severe violence is a clear indication that your pupil is experiencing distress and is in need of reassurance, support and care. Ensure you engage with them in a safe environment where any information they share will be treated confidentially. Help them explore their emotions with word clouds, creative word association and emotion artwork that may indicate how they feel and why. Provide them with other tools and opportunities to express their emotions and process their feelings while maintaining strong and positive relationships with their existing peer group.

Mild and temporary

This is likely to be a vocalization or expression of frustration and may reflect a period of difficulty for your pupil. They may be having a difficult time at home – it could be that there is conflict in the home or significant change. They may be trying to process emotions they haven't experienced before and are unsure how to deal with. Make sure they continue to maintain positive relationships and connections with their peer group and positive interests.

If your pupil is expressing any concerning behaviours, it is important that you work through all nine factors of this framework to ensure you understand the underlying causes and how you can best support them.

Part IV

Communication

12 Managing conversations

This chapter offers some ideas, tools and resources to help you manage communication, initiate conversation and appropriately recognize, reward and support pupils and their parents. As elsewhere in the book, I share the stories of children I have worked with and situations I have faced in schools.

I start with Teresa – much of this handbook has focused more significantly on secondary aged pupils, however we know that difficulties often arise earlier than that. Early intervention has become a commonplace strategy to support children, but sadly it is rarely effectively executed on either an individual or structural level.

> Teresa is in year 5 in school. She has recently moved into the area and lives in the traveller site opposite the school, for fairground travellers. She has attended school for four months in a small two-form entry school that serves the local area. Her attendance is sporadic and she has attended less than half of the available sessions. She sometimes walks to school with other children from her class and is generally well liked by her peers. Teresa is bright, quick to grasp maths concepts and applies them consistently. Her written English is poorer but still meets age-related expectations.
>
> On Friday, she and her female classmates were left alone in the classroom to get changed for PE, with a teacher just outside the room. Teresa proceeded to throw the books and other resources on the floor and tipped over furniture. As the teacher walked in when she heard the noise, she overheard Teresa say to the other girls in the class:
>
> 'Anyone who tells anyone what I've done is a snitch.'

Initiating conversations

Placing yourself in this teacher's shoes, the situation has already arisen and there is the emotional impact of seeing the classroom in a state that is likely to be incredibly upsetting. Primary schoolteachers often give up their time to make their classroom reflect their teaching, but also to make it an exciting and engaging space. Your own connection to the classroom needs to be considered when thinking of how to initiate a conversation which promotes a successful outcome.

There are several aspects that need to be considered with Teresa. One is that it seems apparent that a conversation needs to be initiated with Teresa herself along with the other children in the class who witnessed the event. Another consideration is how to initiate a conversation with Teresa's parents/carers.

The first thing to consider in initiating this conversation is to think about the environment that you find yourself in and how the other children may have experienced the last thing you heard Teresa say before you discovered the mess in the classroom: 'Anyone who tells anyone what I've done is a snitch.' It is likely that trying to talk about this in the public arena of the classroom is not going to be conducive to anyone – either Teresa, you or the other children. You have several options You could:

- request that Teresa comes with you to a different space (either another room or a quieter space in the classroom)
- request that another child in the class comes with you to initiate further discussion
- address the all the girls at the same time to find out what happened.

If we return to the five-stage formula, we realize that we have noticed what has occurred but we don't know why; we haven't moved on to identifying the underlying reasons. In initiating this conversation this needs to be our driving aspect. I find that scripting is a good way of initiating conversations. It builds my own confidence and it is useful to think about certain phrases that will help open up a conversation rather than closing it down.

Children, just like adults, aren't always the most reliable storytellers to tell you what has happened. They have their own values, beliefs and perspectives that shape their narration of events. Children may also be scared of the consequences of events. It may be that Teresa knows this act would bring about a number of things that she does not want: being told off by her parents, being admonished by her teacher and her classmates, and being frustrated with her own behaviour. In managing this conversation, you are likely to want to convey that there were two aspects of her behaviour that were unacceptable – the tipping over of the furniture, and saying that if other children report this they would be 'snitches'. Curtis (2014) describes the use of language plans to promote the behaviour you want to see with children. I am mindful of the power dynamics of some of the things he describes, but there are useful components that can be considered, in particular the planning and reflection of conversations. If we prepare ourselves to respond to children on an individual basis we should be able to develop our confidence in dealing with a range of situations.

For Teresa, I would suggest managing the conversation by reinforcing what you observed and reiterating that you don't know why Teresa said what she said but would like to understand more. Or if you are uncertain about what you heard you can focus on the classroom itself.

- 'Teresa, as I walked in the classroom, I heard you say something that worried me. Do you know what I heard?'

- 'Teresa, I heard you say x when I came into the classroom. Did I hear correctly?'
- 'Teresa, when I left you in the classroom it was tidy. Can you tell me what happened?'

The focus here is on what you noticed and what you observed, but with the request and desire that Teresa tells you more about what happened. Now of course, it may be that Teresa didn't actually make the mess in the classroom (although this seems unlikely) or she may tell you that someone else did it. This is an opportunity to explore and find out more.

Different forms of communication

I see the approach in the previous section as communication which embodies professional curiosity. It aims to find out more rather than shut down discussion. The communication is not punitive but exploratory, and attempts to find out more beyond what you may initially see and hear. However, we know that you don't just communicate through the words you utter, but also by your facial expressions and your body language, and other people may benefit from and respond with communication that incorporates visual and written elements. Below is a review of other forms of communication that you may wish to consider or use.

Facial expressions

Some children may struggle to understand facial expressions – these may be autistic children or those with attachment disorders. Others may need facial expressions to be exaggerated before they can interpret them successfully, or may see threat when it doesn't exist. Our facial expressions may also sometimes conflict with what we are saying (think about a time perhaps where a child has done something that is very funny, but they also need to know the boundaries, and that it isn't acceptable), and this can be confusing for the child who is the recipient of this. Facial expressions can reveal sarcasm, frustration, happiness and anger among a whole host of emotional content.

Body language

Body language is an important component in communication. How we stand, sit, hold our arms, whether or not we avert our gaze are all important ways that we show our own feelings and can be used to attempt to intimidate or put others at ease. There is a balance to be found, looking assured but also unthreatening, especially for children and young people who may have lower thresholds for a threat response. Just in the same way that children are very different, so are we as adults, and also the relationships we have with children develop and change. When you are responding to an individual child, give due consideration to not just what is being said but also how you come across. For some children you may also wish to extend this to using signs or gestures to reiterate what you are saying verbally. For example, putting your hands up with palms facing outward, or getting on your knees for direct eye contact with a primary pupil, or you might let them know they only have two minutes left of play by using hand gestures as well as telling them verbally.

Written communication

Responding individually to children includes using writing as another means of communication. Some staff choose to place the name of a child on the board to let everyone know that their behaviour has been noted but to continue with the delivery of the lesson. It will come as little surprise that I do not advocate this use of written communication as it can be seen as shaming and only involves 'noting' rather than the other stages of the formula of understanding. Having worked in mainstream schools, PRUs and AP, I have seen this used in the past and indeed used it myself. However, I feel it focuses on the negative without detailing what you want to be different.

Instead, in your own individual execution I would suggest trying some things that I later did better, and really enjoyed, which also showed the children I was thinking of them. In my role as Head of Behaviour and Inclusion in a London borough I am sometimes asked to meet with pupils and review their behaviour. On occasions, the child is doing well and is in class, but I don't want them to forget that I am thinking of them. As part of my individual execution I write a little note on a sticky note just saying something along the lines of 'Hey, came to see you today. Mrs Smith told me you were doing super well in class. Brilliant to hear'. Then I tend to draw a smiley face, as even if children can't necessarily access what I have written for whatever reason, they generally know that a smiley face :) means that I am happy. Written communication doesn't have to be formal or long, but it does need to be honest and clear.

Visual communication

Staff in specialist settings are probably more used to using visual forms of communication, but some of these strategies can be incorporated into mainstream and PRU or AP provision. We know that many children may find it difficult to process two-step instructions or to understand complex words. Visual approaches for children who are preverbal may include specific support from speech and language therapists, with the use of augmentative communication systems (ACS) such as the Picture Exchange Communication system (PECS). In these approaches, there is a focus on prompting and reinforcing independent communication. At the most basic phase of communication intervention, there is a single picture or action that can be given to a person to request something. For example, imagine that a child who is preverbal would like to go outside.

They would give or point to the picture of outside, and then this wish is respected by the person who is their communication partner.

Bringing this back to behaviour as a core feature of this handbook, we can understand that not having the words to make your meaning clear, but also having no ability to have your needs understood, can result in challenging behaviour. When we are thinking about responding, we also need to make sure that our meaning is clear, and ACS, in keeping with specific plans for a child, may be used to reinforce what we would like. Fundamentally, we need to ensure that our responses are individually planned for the children we work with to ensure they can be successfully implemented.

Reward and praise

In talking about reward and praise, I am not referring to the use of praise in the context of wider structures (i.e. school behavioural policies) but the everyday reinforcement and support to things we want to see in our classroom. Returning to Teresa and her classmates, how do we respond individually, using praise to support these children in developing positive behaviours in the classroom (even when not in directed activity)? There are a plethora of views relating to praise helping children develop intrinsic motivation (Henderlong and Lepper, 2002) but there is less information about how praise may be used to counteract behavioural issues as and when they occur. Praise is probably best used to counteract issues before they arise and using a 'drip drip ...' effect, bringing gradual changes over time.

However, in terms of responding and individual execution, I would start with saying clearly what you want to hear from the children – which is the truth – phrases such as:

- 'Being truthful is really important. Can you tell me what happened Teresa?'
- 'Thank you very much for telling the truth Teresa'

The first sentence places the behaviour that you want to see at the forefront and reiterates it.

Support from other adults

Some people reading this may have the support of other adults in the classroom. These could be mentors, teaching assistants or volunteers. Others may be able to call for support from other adults. You may find, working in certain settings, that there may be times when you require the support of other adults to continue with teaching. This isn't to discourage the different mechanisms that you may have within the behavioural management of your school, but it is to reiterate the need to ensure that there are opportunities in which you revisit any difficulties that have arisen in school. You may wish to do this with the support of a mentor, senior leader or other pastoral support.

References

Curtis, A. (2014) *Behaviour Language Scripts for Teachers*, 2nd edition. CreateSpace Independent Publishing.

Henderlong, J. and Lepper, M.R. (2002) The effects of praise on children's intrinsic motivation: a review and synthesis, *Psychological Bulletin*, 128(5): 774–95.

13 Individual safeguarding

In responding to the challenges we face in our classes and wider school environments, we have to individually safeguard our own mental health and well-being. We must balance this with the requirements of how we can practically implement, navigate and utilize wider safeguarding processes and policies which are there to protect not just the children we work with, but ourselves as well.

While we may be able to support children's behaviour, understand and support mental health and facilitate equal learning opportunities, we have our limitations. I take it for granted that as you are reading this book you care for the children you work with and want to consider the range of options and ideas on how to support them. While we want to develop healthy professional relationships, it is important that we also delineate clear boundaries for ourselves and the children we work with. This helps us in having time to 'switch off' and not feel overwhelmed, but also supports children in being modelled appropriate relationships and being able to use these strategies in their own personal lives. This is not an easy task – we often hear about the vulnerabilities of children, and that inevitably means that we want to support them in the best way that we can, often developing emotional attachments to the children we work with day in and day out. These feelings are often even more significant in smaller settings such as those seen in PRUs, AP and educational arrangements in children's homes.

In this chapter I explore some of these issues by looking more closely at strategies that provide a mechanism to respond individually to some of the challenges we face in our work contexts.

Looking after yourself

It seems like a simple endeavour, but one that is rarely achieved within the teaching profession: try to have a clear start and end to your work day. If you are able to, and it suits your work/life balance, consider leaving your marking and books at work. Depending on the nature of your living space, you may be able to identify a space in the home that is separate from the normal comings and goings of your family life. You could also avoid loading work emails onto your personal devices such as your phone and laptop. You will then have more control over what you receive and be able to deal with it accordingly.

When a challenge arises – and the likelihood is that it will – create a clear list of your own responsibilities and things you are not responsible for. This will help establish what is within your capacity, power and role to manage, and

124 Communication

Figure 13.1 Looking after yourself

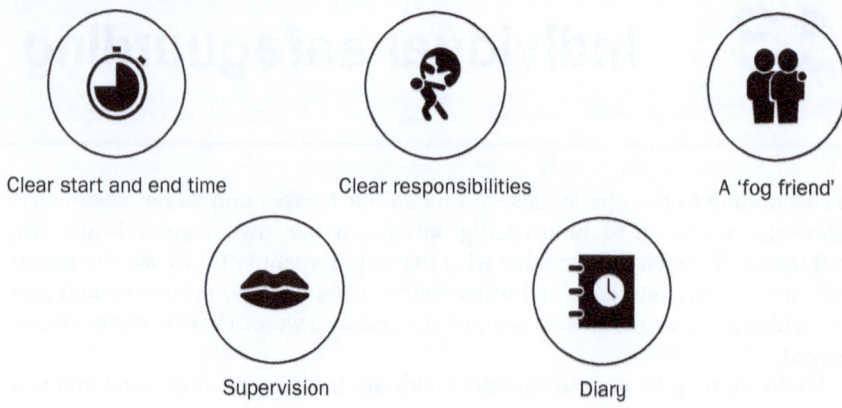

when you may have to delegate or ask others to follow up in relation to specific incidents or issues. It is likely that some of these individuals will be the designated safeguarding lead, headteacher or possibly the Local Area Designated Officer (LADO). In this list, make sure you indicate when you think they ought to be done, and what you will do to follow up and ascertain whether or not what you expected to happen has taken place.

Another strategy may be to appoint a trusted colleague to have as your 'fog friend'. A fog friend refers to the idea that someone is there for you, to see through the 'fog', beyond the challenge in front of you, to help you as well as provide clarity to things when they are difficult. Your fog friend may also sense test a situation and give you an opportunity to reflect and think about it.

For others this may not be possible. You may work in a particularly small environment or not feel confident to speak to other members of staff in your community. You should therefore consider having independent supervision or even counselling sessions when there are particularly challenging times.

It may help to keep a personal diary which maps out some of the events in class (while being mindful about recording children's names and personal details). This can be used to think about any persistent issues or difficulties with children, and how you might think differently about events and consider developing additional strategies to support you.

Looking after others

How we respond as teachers is not just governed by our normal human interactions but also professional standards that we abide by. In the UK, the Department for Education (DfE) sets out a range of specific criteria that make up teachers' standards and headteachers' standards. Those in education are also likely to know about other documentation such as *Keeping Children Safe in*

Education (DfE, 2019) and be mindful of local policies that relate to local safeguarding.

When we think about behaviour, how we individually safeguard and protect children is a driving force behind what we should do, and irrespective of the approach we take this should be a central tenet. We know that the best support we can give to children is carried out *before* a crisis occurs, involves a multidisciplinary approach and draws on our external colleagues such as those in children services and CYPMHS as well as the child's parents/carers.

I have found, working with children and young people, that while you may be able to prepare yourself for the question which frequently appears in interviews, 'what do you do if a child tells you they want to tell you a secret?', the safeguarding aspect is altogether a lot more complex.

In order to explore this subject in more depth, I will start with what I mean by safeguarding, and draw from the National Society for the Protection of Cruelty to Children (NSPCC):

> Safeguarding is the action that is taken to promote the welfare of children and protect them from harm. Safeguarding means: protecting children from abuse and maltreatment, preventing harm to children's health or development, ensuring children grow up with the provision of safe and effective care, taking action to enable all children and young people to have the best outcomes. (NSPCC, 2020)

The NSPCC outlines the need for safeguarding to be not just reactionary but also about taking potentially preventative action to support children in achieving the best outcome.

Throughout, when considering involving others, and when you pass on information or recommend children for multi-agency support or safeguarding, you should not see this as a failure. It is an important part of your role, which you can perform with compassion and confidence.

In looking after others we need to ensure that we abide by national and local policies. The starting point of this is knowing what they say and what they recommend. There have also been significant movements and consideration around ideas of contextual safeguarding. While safeguarding in the past focused on potential harm from significant adults in a child's life such as a parent, contextual safeguarding urges the practitioner to consider the wider environment in a child's life. The Contextual Safeguarding Network defines contextual safeguarding as:

> an approach to understanding, and responding to, young people's experiences of significant harm beyond their families. It recognizes that the different relationships that young people form in their neighbourhoods, schools and online can feature violence and abuse. Parents and carers have little influence over these contexts, and young people's experiences of extra-familial abuse can undermine parent–child relationships. (Contextual Safeguarding Network, 2020)

It is important to consider the wider environment that a child lives in – it isn't just the direct attachments children have but where they live, who they associate with, who lives nearby and all those they pass and engage with on their journeys to and from school. We can see that in order to understand the wider network we must involve others in that child's life, their parents/carers as well as organizations such as those named above.

As part of this we must be clear about our responsibilities within any planning and support with children, how we communicate these responsibilities and how we follow up any actions in a timely fashion.

References

Contextual Safeguarding Network (2020) Contextual Safeguarding website. Available at: https://contextualsafeguarding.org.uk/ (accessed 5 July 2020).

Department for Education (2019) *Keeping Children Safe in Education: Statutory Guidance for Schools and Colleges.* London: DfE.

NSPCC (2020) *Safeguarding Children and Child Protection*, NSPCC website. Available at: https://learning.nspcc.org.uk/safeguarding-child-protection (accessed 5 July 2020).

14 Individual structural preparation

Our current education system in the UK is geared towards mainstream students, the ones that may have difficulties at home but for the most part are going to do ok, behave well in the classroom environment and make friends. Some will go on to the sixth form in their school or choose to go on to colleges, apprenticeships and so on. However, the issue with large organizations that attempt to cater for all children, is that some children won't feel like they fit or belong, that they find things more difficult compared to other children. It may be that they prefer a smaller environment, they don't like moving from teacher to teacher, or even that the journey is arduous. When you are a child there are fewer choices that you can make about the environment in which you learn, compared to work as an adult where there are generally more options or choices in what you do, who you talk to and how you conduct yourself. It is likely that in your schooling career some of the children I have spoken about will resonate with you in particular. It is quite possible that you work with a child who feels like they really struggle in mainstream school and shows continual challenges being in the classroom environment. This chapter explores different options that may be available to that child in the current education system. This isn't to say that I don't agree that the mainstream schooling system should do more to support these children on the margins, but I would prefer to see an education system that offers alternative provision and other options as part of a menu of choice, where no one element is under-resourced or understaffed compared to the next. In exploring these options or thinking about them, I hope that it doesn't seem like you are failing a child, or that they have failed, but you are able to think about all the options and the implications of those options.

In this chapter we explore additional options to mainstream school and how we might consider the alternatives that are available in England. If you are reading this book from an international perspective you may wish to factor in the options available in your own contexts and what might support the children you work with. This chapter specifically looks at wider policy and procedures and how they are experienced from a child's, parent's and teacher's perspective. It also explains the intended functions and purposes of pupil referral units, alternative provision and specialist schools, and the role of local authorities. This will serve as a 'best practice' guide around exclusion and the management of supporting a child's transition to alternative learning provision.

The issue with writing a book is that policy changes over time, which may have an effect on the advice and guidance. Nonetheless, it is helpful to situate our understanding of structural preparation in the wider policy context. To help with this I begin with international policy, which is unlikely to change as much as localized or national policy, and thus provides a potentially more stable starting point. The most obvious international policy which enshrines children's rights to an education are held in the United Nation's Convention on the Rights of the Child:

> Article 28 1. States Parties recognize the right of the child to education, and with a view to achieving this right progressively and on the basis of equal opportunity, they shall, in particular: (a) Make primary education compulsory and available free to all

Yet, in the UK a number of children are excluded, either for a fixed term or permanently. The most recent figures from the Department for Education and Office for National Statistics show that 3 primary school pupils per 10,000 are permanently excluded, and this increases to 20 secondary aged pupils in 10,000. Still, the most frequently cited reason for permanent exclusion is persistent disruptive behaviour. Once a child is excluded from school, whether at primary or secondary level, the local authority as the admissions authority has overall responsibility to organize education for them after the sixth day of exclusion. There is no central data which indicates how many children miss out on 'sixth day provision', only attend part-time or do not have education provision organized for them at all. A number of times in this handbook, from Tommy to Alfie to Fariq, we have heard about children being excluded either fixed-term or permanently. Some of those children access alternative provision in the form of pupil referral units, while others go on to special schools after securing an Education, Health and Care Plan (EHCP).

Revisiting Tommy, at the time of writing this book, you will be relieved to hear that, now 10 years old, he attends a specialist school full-time. After over a year in a PRU he was issued an Education, Health and Care Plan and was diagnosed as being autistic and with pathological demand avoidance (PDA). The point of his specific story was that a lack of enactment of international policy (seeing education as a right), and then national policy (sixth day provision of full-time education, and best endeavours to request an assessment for an EHCP) effectively meant that Tommy was without suitable full-time education for over a year.

I want this handbook to help teachers, senior leaderships and admissions authorities in avoiding a repeat of Tommy's story, one which contained a number of times with no education and disrupted education throughout.

The Special Educational Needs and Disability Code of Practice is statutory guidance for organizations that work with children who have (or who are suspected of having) special educational needs or a disability, issued by the Department for Education and Department of Health and Social Care. The document outlines the associated duties, policies and procedures which specifically relate to Part 3 of the Children and Families Act 2014.

There are two specific sections which I will relate to Tommy's story:

- They must not discriminate for a reason arising in consequence of a child or young person's disability.

- They must make reasonable adjustments, including the provision of auxiliary aids and services, to ensure that disabled children and young people are not at a substantial disadvantage compared with their peers. This duty is anticipatory – it requires thought to be given in advance to what disabled children and young people might require and what adjustments might need to be made to prevent that disadvantage.

In policy and guidance in the UK, there is often a delineation between 'behaviour' and 'mental health'. There have been some amends to rectify this with non-statutory governmental advice in *Mental Health and Behaviour in Schools*, published in 2018 with the aim of supporting children whose mental health issues manifest in behaviour. The document outlines one of its purposes as to:

> identify whether a child or young person's behaviour – disruptive, withdrawn, anxious, depressed or otherwise – may be related to a mental health problem, and how to support them in these circumstances. (DfE, 2018: 3)

However, it is important to recognize that strict delineation between outward behaviours (i.e. disruptive or withdrawn) can hide a multitude of internal turmoil that may be better understood in two-dimensional illustrations that aim to help a teacher visualize the interplay between disruption, withdrawal and so on. This book supports teachers in understanding behaviour beyond that of language, and goes some way towards translating the behaviours that we most struggle to understand. Just as the DfE list above is not an exhaustive or definitive list of behaviours we may see in the classroom or school environment, I aim to cluster behaviours and explain what we may understand by what is being communicated collectively.

Trends in exclusions

In the United Kingdom (UK), exclusions can be broadly split into a number of categories:

- permanent exclusions
- fixed-term exclusions
- lunch-time exclusions.

Each one of these has specific legal ramifications, governance considerations and statutory policy that outlines associated processes. Since the academic year of 1996 the Department for Education has collected statistics relating to permanent exclusions, and then a number of years later on fixed period exclusions. This includes a retrospective 1994/95 collection of data. However, it is noted that the data collection in the earlier years is unreliable (DfE, 2017: 15).

Upon an exclusion a formal notification is submitted to the local authority and then centrally to the DfE. Exclusions must be *lawful, reasonable* and *fair* along with ensuring that practices are not discriminatory relating to protected characteristics (for example disability, or race and ethnicity). There are a number of reasons that a school may exclude a pupil (DfE, 2017: 18):

- bullying
- damage
- drug and alcohol related behaviour
- persistent disruptive behaviour
- physical assault against adult
- physical assault against pupil
- racist abuse
- sexual misconduct
- theft
- verbal abuse/threatening behaviour against adult
- verbal abuse/threatening behaviour against pupil.

Throughout the years of data collection, persistent disruptive behaviour remains the main reason given for both fixed-term and permanent exclusion. In the last year of recording (data is collected retrospectively the following year), the number of fixed-term exclusions for children with persistent disruptive behaviour has increased by 10 per cent from the previous year, while permanent exclusions for the same reason have decreased slightly by 2 per cent (DfE, 2019 – main text).

It is a clear concern that children with certain demographics are more likely to be excluded; a boy who is black African-Caribbean and has free school meals (FSM) is more likely to be permanently excluded compared to a white girl. If you are identified as having special educational needs or as a looked after child this further increases the risk of exclusion.

We must understand, unpick and counteract some of our structural prejudices relating to the Eurocentric curriculum, a curriculum that doesn't feel meaningful for the children who come to our classes, while maintaining high expectations. We must also consider why it is that children who live in poverty and come from certain ethnic groups are more likely to be excluded. What is it about our structural systems that re-enact rather than disrupt these cycles of poverty?

What are the current options in school?

In this section I begin to reveal how the different practices in school can affect children on an individual level. It is no surprise that schools can apply a number of options for children whose behaviour is deemed undesirable and when there are infractions of rules. However, these are often in response to behaviour rather than systemic structures in school to provide an inclusive environment where children's needs are met and understood. The DfE asks that schools publish their behaviour policy and I have included some examples below. Some schools have showcased their practices in their literature and in these instances I refer to the name of the school. When a school has only published information on their own website under their behaviour policy, I have omitted the name and key demographic details.

Zero tolerance

Alongside concerns relating to poor behaviour there have also been concerns about a perceived lack of progress and achievement in the education system. With this comes different policies, strategies and approaches on how to improve aspects which are seen to lead to a strain on progress and attainment. These include drives to improve attendance at school and promotion of positive behaviour and curtailment of poor behaviour. A more regimented approach is offered by schools such as Michaela Community School, which is detailed more specifically in their book *Battle Hymn of the Tiger Teachers* (Birbalsingh, 2016). The Michaela Community School behaviour policy outlines a system of demerits, referral (some schools may refer to this as isolation) and centralized detention. This approach, as argued by the headteacher Katherine Birbalsingh, is a systematic way of promoting positive behaviour and high expectations of all children irrespective of their backgrounds.

It is simplistic to say that zero tolerance sits in opposition to trauma-informed approaches, but they are often discussed as polarized understandings of discipline. One approach for Michaela Community School is 'SLANT', an acronym that stands for

S – Sit up
L – Listen
A – Answer questions
N – Never interrupt
T – Track the speaker

It is interesting to note how this approach fits in with attempting to understand the meaning behind the behaviour; how we may identify needs, understand them and successfully respond in a way that is conducive to both the individual child and the wider school community.

Alternative provision and pupil referral units

Alternative provision statutory guidance for local authorities outlines the definition of AP:

> education arranged by local authorities for pupils who, because of exclusion, illness or other reasons, would not otherwise receive suitable education; education arranged by schools for pupils on a fixed period exclusion; and pupils

being directed by schools to off-site provision to improve their behaviour. (DfE, 2013: 3)

Alternative provision is a general term which includes a range of different educational arrangements for children. These are reflected in the Forgotten Children report indicating that:

> Alternative provision (AP) is a broad term and imperfectly describes a wide variety of types of school or educational settings. Our inquiry scope included Pupil Referral Units (PRUs); alternative provision academies and free schools; hospital schools; and alternative provision delivered by charities and other organizations as well as independent or unregistered schools. (House of Commons, 2018: 7)

Some children may be excluded from mainstream schooling and the local authority arrange for their education at alternative provision such as a pupil referral unit, or in an academy AP provision. Others may remain on the roll at their mainstream school but be directed to education off-site (parents do not have rights to appeal this decision), while other children may access education in a medical PRU or AP, which traditionally will take children with a range of health needs such as anxiety, school refusal, obsessive compulsive disorder and so on. Sometimes children may be admitted to hospital and their education in the hospital school may be designated as a special school (e.g. the provision on offer at Great Ormond Street Hospital) or as a satellite of a larger PRU provision.

Essentially, the arrangements in AP vary across the UK, and as such so may the resources on offer, the outcomes and the cohort of children who attend the provision (Timpson, 2019). The perceptions of PRUs and AP are often negative in the wider media, with terms such as 'sin bin' being used to describe them. There are significant concerns that 42 per cent of adults in the prison population have self-reported being excluded from school (Gill, 2007). Additionally media reporting, while it quite rightly should be highlighting concerns about children's outcomes in all provision, often fails to recognize the host of needs that children may present with before they are excluded from school.

Hospital schools and medical pupil referral units

There is little discussed in the wider literature about the role of hospital schools and medical PRUs, although some national organizations are attempting to address this balance (for example the National Association for Hospital Education and Units United). Each local authority retains the responsibility for arranging education for children who are too unwell to attend school (Department for Health and Social Care, 2015). While the local authority and education providers have no oversight of admissions into hospitals (these are clinical and medical decisions), they are in a unique position to support children while they are accessing medical treatment.

Hospital schools and medical PRUs include well-known organizations such as Great Ormond Street Hospital, which is registered as a special school, as well as smaller arrangements made by the local authority to support tuition such as home tuition services.

Children accessing such services have a range of needs, some of which are life-limiting and life-threatening such as leukaemia, complex genetic conditions, kidney failure and so on. Others may need such support as they recover from traumatic injuries or surgery. However, the vast majority are those with psychiatric and mental health issues. These include children with depression, psychosis, anorexia nervosa and OCD among others. Some of the latter may be educated in Tier 4 inpatient psychiatric services, while others may be supported in their homes, local communities or specific PRUs or AP for children with health needs.

In 2018 the Department for Education announced funding for a number of AP innovation projects. One such project run by Northamptonshire Hospital and Outreach Education secured £522,142 to implement a project to support children returning to school. The focus was on the use of telepresence robots as the eyes and ears of a child when they couldn't attend school. The AV1 telepresence avatar would be in the classroom while the child would be in their home, hospital bed, or hospital school controlling the avatar from a tablet. This research, titled 'Assessing the Efficacy of Telepresence Robots', looked to develop innovative practices to improve children's attendance at school, as well as look at factors relating to their sense of belonging to their school, and whether or not 'warm technology' could help to reduce feelings of loneliness that can occur when a child is receiving treatment for medical needs.

References

Birbalsingh, K. (2016) *Battle Hymn of the Tiger Teachers: The Michaela Way*. London: John Catt Educational Ltd.

Department for Education (2013) *Alternative Provision: Statutory Guidance for Local Authorities*. London: DfE. Available at: https://assets.publishing.service.gov.uk/government/uploads/system/uploads/attachment_data/file/268940/alternative_provision_statutory_guidance_pdf_version.pdf (accessed 9 November 2020).

Department for Education (2017) *Guide to Exclusion Statistics*. London: DfE.

Department for Education (2018) *Alternative Provision Innovation Fund: Successful Applicants*. Available at: https://www.gov.uk/government/publications/alternative-provision-innovation-fund/alternative-provision-innovation-fund-successful-applicants (accessed 23 August 2020).

Department for Education (2019) *Permanent and Fixed Period Exclusions in England 2017 to 2018*. Available at: https://www.gov.uk/government/statistics/permanent-and-fixed-period-exclusions-in-england-2017-to-2018 (accessed 27 July 2020).

Department for Health and Social Care (2015) *Hospital Education: A Guide for Health Professionals*. Available at https://www.gov.uk/government/publications/hospital-education-a-guide-for-health-services/hospital-education-a-guide-for-health-services (accessed 7 June 2020).

Gill, K. (2017) Making The Difference: Breaking the link between school exclusion and social exclusion, IPPR. Available at: http://www.ippr.org/publications/making-the-difference (accessed 11 December 2020).

House of Commons (2018) *Forgotten Children: Alternative Provision and the Scandal of Ever Increasing Exclusions.* London: House of Commons.

National Association of Hospital Education. NAHE website. Available at: https://nahe.org.uk/ (accessed 7 June 2020).

No Isolation (2020) No Isolation website. Available at: https://www.noisolation.com/uk (accessed 7 June 2020).

Timpson, E. (2019) *Timpson Review of School Exclusion.* London: DfE.

15 Responding: structural execution

In working with children and young people in the education system, especially those with significant needs, it can feel that we are trapped by its policies, processes and rigid structures. In initial teacher training it may be that while there has been significant support with teaching, pedagogy and a broad brush understanding of supporting children with significant needs, it would also be helpful to know about the various pathways and support to help children access external support and how to engage with those various agencies.

Parents/carers are a key part of any decision-making. They are part of the wider structures, as individual parents of children you work with but also as the wider community. In developing good relationships with parents you enable potentially difficult conversations to take place. There are often questions around how you engage with parents/carers about their children's education. I think it needs to be taken into account that we all come with our own history and views of education, our own perspectives and personal background. Parents/carers themselves may have had poor experiences of school and this could shape your interaction with them on a daily basis, or even a lack of interaction or interest in their child's schooling. When thinking about how to engage parents, this needs to come from a position in which you are interested in their views and what they have to say, like the children who you work with. Some areas around communication are discussed in more detail in Chapter 12, but in supporting parents we have another avenue of encouraging structurally the behaviour of the children in our schools. In providing clear information about expectations, our aims are to prevent exclusion. We want children to feel like they belong to the wider school community, and in making this happen, we want their parents/carers to feel the same. Visibility is important, and so is being available. In thinking about different avenues for support, our pupils' parents need to be able to understand why additional organizations or approaches are being used.

Different avenues for support

We have spoken in depth about different approaches that we may have in individually responding to a child's needs. However, there may be times when looking at additional structural options could be a way to benefit the individual

Figure 15.1 Structural responses

Nurture groups   Emotional literacy support assistants (ELSA)   Mentoring   Speech and language interventions

child. Different areas will vary in their access to support, but I have looked at some options below to help you consider what may be helpful.

Nurture groups

The idea of being nurtured brings about images of mother and child, a close relationship, kindness and positive regard between two people. In trying to move beyond the concept of nurture groups (which I do outline below) I asked others about what they understood by the term 'nurture'. These are some of their responses:

- to love and care for another
- to provide support
- to take someone under your wing
- nurture is all about warmth, relationships, trust and unconditional positive regard.

In the context of education and wider policy the term 'nurture', and specifically nurture groups, has been evident in education in the last fifty years, developed from the ideas of Margaret Boxall who worked in the London Borough of Hackney. She had ongoing concerns about children struggling with their behaviour in school. She saw nurture groups as a short-term intervention to support children who demonstrated difficulties in the class. Mary Warnock commented on these groups as 'compensatory measures' for children who were seen as not socially or emotionally well developed. It is notable that many of the children in the first cohort of nurture groups were first generation immigrants of the Windrush generation – i.e. their parents had come to Britain to fill the labour shortfall after the Second World War. Nurture groups still exist in the schooling community; some are in a child's home school, others are accessed in a different mainstream school as a way of pooling resources in the local community. Typically a child will attend for the majority of their time in the nurture group for six to eight weeks, while maintaining a contact with their home school by attending that school on a given day each week. The idea is that the child does not lose their attachment or their important relationships in their home school and this will effectively support their return to full-time provision there.

Emotional literacy support assistants (ELSA)

ELSA refers to a teaching assistant who has been given specific training on core areas beyond the national curriculum. The approach is often trauma-informed and based around the development of a child's social skills, their ability to manage anger, make friends and develop their self-esteem. ELSA training is often solution-focused (what can be done) rather than punitive. Local authorities sometimes provide training for schools to support the development of ELSA staff. ELSA and nurture groups are closely linked, with ELSA staff often being a significant resource within nurture groups as well as in the wider school. Some ELSA staff may provide additional support for a child in class, while others may run specific groups and interventions for children, depending on the nature of the school and their access to separate space and resources to run such activities.

Mentoring

Mentoring has a long history of providing a structural response to supporting individual relationships between student and teacher. The term mentoring has been used to describe a relationship between an individual with more experience and a 'novice'. Mentoring as a term is wide ranging and diversity of relationships can be categorized as that which encompasses mentoring (Dawson, 2014). Marino et al. (2000) succinctly state that mentoring is when 'an adult or elder peer is paired with an at-risk youth with the aim to develop a trusting and supporting relationship, thus improving youth well-being'. There are a range of different types of mentoring that are reported to have a positive effect in a range of areas of a child's life but there are higher rates of confidence in mentoring that takes place in the community rather than at home (Herrera et al., 2000). It is no surprise that positive relationships between mentor and mentee are cited as a core feature of better outcomes for young people (Herrera et al., 2000: 25). Mentoring in particular has been seen as a positive structural response to supporting children who are deemed as being at risk (Marino et al., 2020). At risk may include reports of low self-esteem, lack of connectedness to school, and substance misuse. Some of the practical interventions of the mentoring relationships included visiting museums, galleries, parks and other activities.

Mentoring can be a helpful intervention in supporting children in considering their decision making but needs to be seen within the wider contextual situation that the child may be in. The mentoring relationship needs to feed into the wider school systems and provide real opportunity for the child or young person to feel safe in talking through difficulties in a space which is non-judgemental, engaging and building up a relationship with a trusted adult.

Speech and language

There is a growing body of evidence that speech and language difficulties have a fundamental effect on children's wider achievement: academically, in their relationship with peers and even increased likelihood in being involved in the criminal justice system (Hartshorne, 2009: 6–7). In understanding these concerns Hartshorne considers two specific areas of difficulties, one of which is seen as transient difficulties with language, the other persistent difficulties (Hartshorne, 2009: 4). In addressing the difficulties their recommendation includes the structural response of specific early intervention programmes which include clear descriptive targets in smaller milestones as seen within previous P Scales (attainment goals for some children identified as having special educational needs).

Some schools, particularly primary, have intervention groups which build upon these structural interventions and may focus on core skills such as listening and attention, receptive and expressive language and pre-learning of vocabulary. Sobel (2018) characterises pre- and over-learning of vocabulary as 'exposing the student to words and ideas that are about to come up in the lesson, and going over them again after the lesson'.

In developing this approach the aim is to support a child in a language-rich environment, where increasing their knowledge of words that they may not have been previously exposed to is a key feature of their education.

Outside agencies and structures

There are a number of outside agencies that may support children using a multidisciplinary approach. We know that other disciplines may provide additional training, ideas and resources that we can draw upon to support children.

In-year fair access protocols

Each local authority must have fair access protocols – these may be referred to by slightly different names, such as an inclusion panel or using the acronym FAP. The purpose of fair access protocols is to ensure that children who are not on the roll at a school, are outside of the normal admission period (i.e. think of a September start for schools in England) and are deemed as most vulnerable, are found a school as quickly as possible (DfE, 2012: 3). Fair access panels can be formal panels that sit with key senior leaders from a school, or can be based in the local authority to make decisions as the admission authority. They are often concerned about children who may have a history of exclusion, who are newly arrived to the local authority area or have been released from a custodial sentence. In-year fair access panels may also discuss managed moves. In a managed move, a child remains on the roll at their previous school but starts attending another for a period of time to see whether or not a fresh start will help and reduce the risk of exclusion. Hutchinson and Crenna-Jennings reflect on concerns about unexplained pupil moves in the context of managed moves, saying:

> We also estimated how many unexplained exits to different schools might be considered 'managed moves.' These are, typically, moves that take place

> from one school to another without an official exclusion taking place and are brokered locally by headteachers and the local authority. While these moves might be in the best interest of the pupil, there is no transparency over the cause or prevalence of these moves either locally or nationally. Processes vary across the country and we cannot observe from the national data whether families are supportive of these moves or not. We therefore classify all managed moves as unexplained. (Hutchinson and Crenna-Jennings, 2019: 9)

In drawing on local approaches it is important to return back to both the XY axis and the five-stage formula to really understand what is driving some of the more difficult things that you are seeing in the school community. Would a 'fresh start' really help to unpick some of the things that a child is finding difficult, or merely replicate them in a different environment? If a fresh start is what a child needs, how can things be amended in their current placement to make this happen? Moving from school to school may have unintended consequences such as the child feeling like they don't belong in the new environment.

Multi-agency safeguarding hubs

Many areas have established multi-agency safeguarding hubs (MASH). These were developed to support the sharing of information across agencies after several serious incident reviews saw communication as a key area to be addressed (Home Office, 2014). MASH are often co-located, with the idea that not only can external staff have an open door approach to communication and advice, but the hubs can also prevent duplication of information and ensure that a range of perspectives is available to help support a child and minimize risk.

Child and Young People's Mental Health Services (CYPMHS)

CYPMHS is part of the National Health Service (NHS) and aims to provide assessment and treatment for children who demonstrate mental health needs – through the behaviour they exhibit at school, home or in the community – or for children who have difficult thoughts and feelings. CYPMHS supports children with a range of psychiatric needs, some of them covered in this book, but including clinical depression, victims of abuse, schizophrenia, bipolar and eating disorders. CYPMHS is a multidisciplinary service but with a clinical focus, which includes psychiatrists, psychologists, nurses and social workers. You can access CYPMHS in a number of ways such as a referral from a child's general practitioner, their school or other specialist services such as the youth offending service or social services. More recently some CYPMHS services have moved on to more hub-based models offering in-school support, or working in third-sector charities. CYPMHS is also referred to as child and adolescent mental health services (CAMHS).

Home and hospital tuition services

When we talk about exclusions we often forget to talk about the children who are marginalized and excluded because they are unable to attend school due to medical needs. In 2014 the DfE published guidance on *Supporting Pupils with Medical Conditions at School*. This document outlines the statutory responsibilities of the school and governing body in making arrangements for children with health needs in school. However, there is also recognition that for some children arrangements in school may not be appropriate or possible:

> LAs are responsible for arranging suitable full-time education for children of compulsory school age who, because of illness, would not receive suitable education without such provision. This applies whether or not the child is on the roll of a school and whatever the type of school they attend. It applies to children who are pupils in Academies, Free Schools, special schools and independent schools as well as those in maintained schools. (DfE, 2013: 9)

Your local authority should have a named officer who is responsible for arrangements for children who are unable to access school, and should provide you with details on how to refer the child to receive support while they are unwell or receiving treatment for a medical illness, for either mental or physical health needs.

Third-sector organizations

The third sector refers to organizations which are non-profit making and non-government. These may include charities, community groups and volunteers.

Depending on your location you may have particular third-sector charities that may be able to support children individually. These include organizations such as St Giles Trust, Catch22, Barnardo's, etc. They may offer support such as mentoring, opportunities for apprenticeships or other interventions. When you are looking at third-sector opportunities, ensure that you approach any request for support in the same way that you would look at employment of a member of staff. Pay due regard to any safeguarding practices that you would normally, with the additional understanding that some charities will intentionally work with individuals who have a history of criminal activity.

References

Barnardo's website. Available at: https://www.barnardos.org.uk/ (accessed 8 July 2020).
Catch22 website. Available at: https://www.catch-22.org.uk/ (accessed 8 July 2020).
Dawson, P. (2014) Beyond a definition: toward a framework for designing and specifying mentoringmodels,*EducationalResearcher*,43(3):137–145.doi:10.3102/0013189X14528751
Department for Education (2012) *Fair Access Protocols: Principles and Processes*. London: DfE. [Online.]
Department for Education (2013) *Education for Children with Health Needs who cannot attend School because of Health Needs*, DfE website. Available at: https://www.gov.uk/government/publications/education-for-children-with-health-needs-who-cannot-attend-school (accessed 1 November 2020).

Department for Education (2014) *Supporting Pupils with Medical Conditions at School*, DfE website. Available at: https://www.gov.uk/government/publications/supporting-pupils-at-school-with-medical-conditions-3 (accessed 1 November 2020).

Department for Education (2017) Performance – P Scale – attainment targets for pupils with special educational needs. Available at:https://assets.publishing.service.gov.uk/government/uploads/system/uploads/attachment_data/file/903590/Performance_-_P_Scale_-_attainment_targets_for_pupils_with_special_educational_needs_June_2017.pdf (accessed 14 December 2020).

ELSA support website. Available at: https://www.elsa-support.co.uk/ (accessed 1 July 2020).

Hartshorne, M. and Major, G. (2009) Using Action Learning Sets to change practice in supporting pupil's speech, language and communication in secondary schools at www.thecommunicationtrust.org.uk

Herrera, C., Sipe, C., McClanahan, W. et al. (2000) Mentoring school-age children: relationship development in community-based and school-based programs.

Home Office (2014) *Multi Agency Working and Information Sharing Project: Final Report*. London: Home Office. Available at: https://assets.publishing.service.gov.uk/government/uploads/system/uploads/attachment_data/file/338875/MASH.pdf (accessed 16 November 2020).

Hutchinson, J. and Crenna-Jennings, W. (2019) *Unexplained Pupil Exits*. London: Education Policy Institute. Available at: https://epi.org.uk/wp-content/uploads/2019/10/Unexplained-pupil-moves_LAs-MATs_EPI-2019.pdf (accessed 20 July 2020).

Marino, C., Santinello, M., Lenzi, M. et al. (2020) Can mentoring promote self-esteem and school connectedness? An evaluation of the Mentor-UP Project, *Psychosocial Intervention*, 29(1): 1–8. https://doi.org/10.5093/pi2019a13

Nurture UK (2019) *Nurture at 50: A Timeline*, Nurture UK website. Available at: https://www.nurtureuk.org/50-years-nurture/nurture-50-timeline (accessed 7 July 2020).

Sobel, D. (2018) Teaching interventions: Pre and over learning. Available at https://www.sec-ed.co.uk/best-practice/teaching-interventions-pre-and-over-learning/ (accessed 14 December 2020).

St Giles Trust website. Available at: https://www.stgilestrust.org.uk/ (accessed 7 July 2020).

16 Structural safeguarding

People may assume that once a child is excluded from school, the teacher returns to a class which is less disruptive and more peaceful. Teachers may hold the hope that they can now concentrate on their less disruptive pupils and embrace a more peaceful classroom while focusing on their high achieving students. However, the reality is that many teachers carry the thoughts of those children for many years afterwards and have concern for them and an interest in their future. They wonder how they are doing and hope that they are doing well. This is perhaps one of the hardest factors to consider. Individually, we must safeguard ourselves by developing a clear understanding of what the implications are of a number of structures, not involving ourselves with individual pupils, but making sure there are structural measures that ensure every child is supported, and provided with the best support and outcomes.

In this area I look at some of the structural issues that may arise and their implications for children. I begin with issues that relate to pupil movement, what is meant by 'off-rolling' and consider the perverse incentives that relate to schools using exclusionary practices. I also look at how our responses to behaviour are monitored.

On roll, off roll and dual-rolled

When a child is admitted to a school they are placed 'on roll', and if a child moves to another school they are generally taken off the roll of that school and placed on roll at the next. Some children may be 'dual-rolled', whereby they are on the roll of two different provisions, one designated as the main roll and the other as the subsidiary roll. The subsidiary roll is likely to be a PRU, AP or in some instances a hospital school while a child has treatment as an inpatient.

'Off-rolling' is a term which has been increasingly used to express concerns about children leaving school. It relates to a child being taken off the school's roll and may or may not appear on the roll of another school. A definition is provided by the Education Policy Institute:

> Over recent years, there has been rising concern about unexplained exits from English schools – often focusing on 'off-rolling' as a subset of school exits deemed to be in the interests of the school and not the child. The concern has been that schools – under pressure from government and other accountability targets – have been 'unloading' more vulnerable pupils, without actually formally excluding them. It is difficult to assess the scale and prevalence

of any such activity, because detailed data about the reasons for school exits is not recorded at a national level. (Hutchinson and Crenna-Jennings, 2019: 7)

In this paper exploring unexplained pupil exits, there is consideration of what the driving forces are behind these movements between schools. Hutchinson and Crenna-Jennings express concerns that the purpose of moving these children is not necessarily clear, and nor are the wishes of the parents, or whether or not they feel pressured into the move. As part of their recommendations they explain that there needs to be a drive to understand how wider structural policymaking influences and affects children's experiences of schooling:

Government needs to recognise the complex causes of behaviour difficulties in its policies and guidance. These include trauma from abuse or neglect and attachment problems, the effects of material poverty such as hunger and inadequate housing, parental stress and mental health difficulties, and unsupported special educational needs and disabilities. (Hutchinson and Crenna-Jennings, 2019: 4)

Essentially, how we respond to structural issues affects the children we are working with, but we are unable to really understand the effect of some of these wider policymaking decisions.

References

Hutchinson, J. and Crenna-Jennings, W. (2019) *Unexplained Pupil Exits*. London: Education Policy Institute. Available at: https://epi.org.uk/wp-content/uploads/2019/10/Unexplained-pupil-moves_LAs-MATs_EPI-2019.pdf (accessed 20 July 2020).

17 Communicating clearly

In nearly all roles that involve working with children, there is a requirement to correspond with those internally (such as the senior leadership team, special educational needs coordinator (SENCO)), as well as external stakeholders such as parents/carers, CYPMHS, social services and other schools. In this chapter, we look at different approaches to communicating clearly with a range of organizations – from completing incident report forms, to expressing a concern about a behaviour, to managing meetings successfully, keeping the child at the centre of our thinking.

Communicating clearly is not an easy task and shouldn't be taken for granted. If it was simple then it would not appear as a recurring feature in serious case reviews that aim to understand what happened when a child has died. The recommendation that there should be better communications, both internal and external to an organization, is something that is often cited and yet is revisited time and time again when it comes to the next serious case review. Clear communication is a fundamental, and not something that should be overlooked. How we talk to others, explain our perspectives and make plans can make huge differences to the outcomes of children and therefore this deserves a space to reflect on it in this book. We also look at some pitfalls that I have seen and explain why these become problematic when attempting to support a child.

Paperwork

One thing that people often forget when writing up paperwork is that the person the document is about may see it. Even in instances when it feels like a private email the way we speak about individuals needs to remain professional and considerate of the individual's needs. Not just because it is the *right* thing to do, but also legislation relating to General Data Protection Regulation (GDPR) enshrines the rights of people to see a copy of any information relating to them. The other thing to consider is that documentation in a student's file will follow with them and people may read the document to understand what it is saying. I have often seen such phrases such as 'Billy acted *inappropriately* in class'. In trying to unpick what this means, *inappropriate* does not tell us what the behaviour was; it could be looking out of the window, or refusing to work, and while you would expect a greater level of detail it may imply that the child has sworn at a teacher. Communicating clearly should be about being explicit in the language that we use to explain the behaviour of others. For example, if a child has sworn at you, while it may feel uncomfortable saying 'Billy called me a bitch', this does mean that it is clear what has been said, rather than having to debate it later on in further meetings and discussions. Ultimately, paperwork can be picked up several months later, and it needs to give a clear sense of what has occurred without anyone having to speak to the person directly, especially as people may have moved on with their specific roles.

Report writing

When writing a report it is helpful to have a clear idea about who the intended audience is, as well as who else may read the document. Is this a school report, intended for a parent/carer? Or is the report aimed at an external stakeholder to request access to additional resources? If it is for parents, do they have previous poor experiences of schooling which may influence how they read and understand the document? Is the document written in a way that is meaningful, clear and without jargon?

We may have all been in positions as a child or with our own children where we see a report that looks remarkably like one of our friend's reports or another child's. Remember it is no surprise that parents share what has been written about their child, especially when it is something to be proud of. So while you may use certain phrases or sentence starters, they talk about the child that you are commenting on.

When report writing you will generally be given guidelines or even key statements to use to describe a child and whether or not they are reaching specific milestones or progressing. In doing this be mindful of stereotypes that you may be perpetuating by what you write. For example, are you acknowledging and reinforcing stereotypes that girls should be quiet and passive in their learning while boys should be more engaged in physical activities?

If your report is to an outside agency, take some time to think about what you would like the outcome of the document to be. It is not just communicating a child's progress, but might be about accessing additional support. You want to be honest, while signifying your concerns about a particular behaviour. Here you may wish to draw upon the XY axis, and rather than vague phrases such as 'Andrew is angry', start providing further detail so that someone is able to understand what that anger is driven by and perhaps where additional services may be able to support him.

Behavioural incident reports

Your school is likely to have specific documentation that requires completion centrally for any issues relating to behaviour that occur. These are usually electronic-based systems such as CPOMS (Child Protection Online Management System) or SIMS (School Information Management Systems). Behavioural incident reports are important documents, and while it may not seem important to complete the data it can give an organization a clearer idea when issues may arise. For example, are incidents peppered throughout the week or always on a Monday? Are they just before lunch-time or when it's time to go home? Or are

Figure 17.1 Five stages of responding

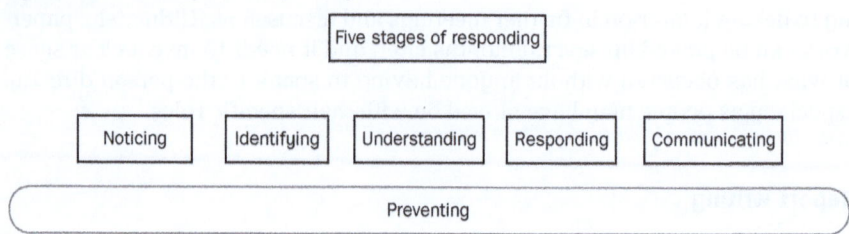

they always in a maths lesson? In communicating clearly it is helpful to include a level of detail that you may not realize is important, but someone else that may be looking at issues from a wider overview can make links to the larger data set created.

Behaviour incident reports also have the benefit of helping you use the five-stage framework. If we return to the diagram in Figure 17.1, what we may write in a behavioural incident report may initially be limited to noticing and responding. What did we notice prior to the event (essentially the antecedent), what happened, how did we understand it and how did we respond? For example, consider the following three examples of details relating to the same incident:

- Emma acted inappropriately in maths. 30-minute detention.
- In the maths class today, Emma threw a rubber at Phillip without provocation. 30-minute detention after school.
- In maths today, I noticed that Emma seemed annoyed. She sat in a different seat to normal. As I began teaching the class and introduced the topic, Emma threw a rubber at Phillip's head. I spoke to Emma and she said she did it 'because Phillip is a dick'. I responded by reminding her of the behavioural policy and reiterating appropriate behaviour before sanctioning her to a 30-minute detention after school. I informed her parents with a phone call home and explained.

The difference in the three reports is limited to a number of extra lines. It is not helpful to necessarily put your own emotional content into the behavioural report about the student (although you may of course wish to speak to your colleagues directly about this) but it should give a clear sense of what occurred. If I picked up the first behavioural incident report, 'Emma acted inappropriately in maths. 30-minute detention', I would be no clearer about what actually occurred in the class. I wouldn't have known there was another child involved and nor would I have a sense that there is something potentially troublesome in the relationship between Phillip and Emma. Having these details means that I can start planning from a wider systems approach rather than responding each time an incident occurs. It is noteworthy that, as a pastoral leader or anyone with responsibility for behaviour, you are likely to see the first and second comments routinely. While it may save the individual teacher time initially, it is unlikely to save their colleagues time later as they try to unravel the initial situation.

If we then review the incident report we can see the five stages in more detail highlighted below. Now, a lot of the understanding happens outside of this behaviour report but there are elements of it occurring:

> In maths today, I *noticed* that Emma seemed annoyed. She sat in a different seat to normal. As I began teaching the class and introduced the topic, Emma threw a rubber at Phillip's head [*noticed*]. I spoke to Emma and she said she did it 'because Phillip is a dick' [*understanding*]. I *responded* by reminding her of the behavioural policy and reiterating appropriate behaviour before sanctioning her to a 30-minute detention after school. I informed her parents with a phone call home and explained [*communicating*].

Telephone conversations

With parents

The most important thing to highlight is: do not only ring home with bad news. No one wants to hear from their child's school for the first time because something untoward has happened that means you are forced to talk to them. We know that some parents/carers may have poor experiences of the education system themselves, or may have their own difficulties. Building relationships with parents is a key factor in developing a better relationship with children. If you notice a child doing something well in your class and you have the time for a three-minute conversation at the end of the day, you could ring up and just say:

> Hello Mrs Hogg, do you have time to talk? I just want to let you know that Charlotte worked really hard in English today. I was really impressed with the way she grasped the poetic devices in the poem in Mrs Tilscher's class. She probably won't tell you about it but maybe ask her.

Or if you think this may be too much information, shorten it down to just simply 'Hello Mrs Hogg, do you have time to talk? I just want to let you know that Charlotte worked really hard in English today. I was really impressed with her. She probably won't tell you about it but maybe if you ask her?'

The conversation does not have to be long, but it does require you knowing about Charlotte and it needs to be honest. It means that when Charlotte next comes to your class she will know you've spoken to her mum (potentially preventing future issues) but it also means that if Charlotte is finding things difficult, then Mrs Hogg will remember what you said at that time and is more likely to listen.

With external agencies

When making a telephone call with an external professional, consider what would be a good time to call them. Some staff in schools may be on site early, but will be teaching during the day. Other professionals may catch up with phone calls after clinic hours or lesson time. Generally speaking, when making a phone call to an external agency be prepared to have to leave a message. Just as you are unlikely to be in the office, available to take a phone call, they will have the same issue. I describe it as 'phone call ping-pong', where you keep leaving one another messages until that magical moment when you actually get to speak to the person directly.

Also consider whether or not the conversation can take place by email or remote conferencing that can be booked in advance. It may only be a ten-minute call that is required but when you are rushing from class to class, or person to person, having a specific time in which you can do this can be helpful. When you telephone, make sure you are clear what the purpose of the phone call is, how much time you may need to set aside, and if possible when you are leaving a message ask for the recipient's email address or leave your own, as some outside professionals may not be willing to give contact details like this without knowing clearly who the recipient is.

Face-to-face meetings

Face-to-face meetings can happen for a variety of reasons – it may be due to normal teacher/parent reporting or could be due to a specific incident. When planning face-to-face meetings remember that we all have different priorities, and what feels important to you may not have the same urgency for others. Especially when planning meetings with parents, be mindful that for them this may be yet another meeting they attend for their child and another meeting about something that is potentially negative.

Consider the family's access to resources – for some parents/carers it may be easier to meet you on the school site. Especially in primary schools, where the children tend to live closer and only a walk away, having a meeting on the school grounds may be preferable for all concerned. However, there are occasions where you might find it trickier to schedule a meeting. Just like working with the children we have discussed throughout the book, consider moving beyond noticing to identifying and understanding. What is stopping this meeting happening on the school grounds? Is it that they don't feel comfortable with schools in general because of their own experience? Is it that they see the meeting as pointless because they don't know what to do any more? Is it because they are disabled and leaving the house presents significant difficulties? Do they have a newborn baby and the thought of getting on the bus to attend a meeting six miles away just feels like a mammoth task? In trying to understand what the underlying reasons are you may be able to make adjustments to your normal practice and think of a solution where you all feel comfortable for a face-to-face meeting.

In the PRU and AP sector, I have had the opportunity to meet many of the children at their homes; I have seen their parents/carers and their pets too. I have had the chance to meet their siblings and wider families. At first this feels quite alien, as if you are not careful it can feel like an imposition into someone's home. Remember that this is their space, and think how you might feel if a professional went into your own home.

In arranging face-to-face meetings at a person's home, ensure that you have a robust lone working policy, which includes someone knowing where you are, that there aren't significant risks in visiting the home that can't be mitigated, and that the meeting is diarized for your school to recognize. Ultimately, make sure the face-to-face meeting is not for your convenience but for benefit of the child or young person.

Once the meeting is arranged, it is important that the difference between the purposes of different meetings is recognized. This is acknowledged by your demeanour and what you say. In attending meetings where a child has been permanently excluded, or when a child is returning to school after a fixed-term exclusion, I always acknowledge that no parent wants to be called to this type of meeting. Recognize this at the beginning, signpost that you know this isn't easy – it doesn't need to take up the majority of the meeting, just a moment: 'I know Mrs King that we are not meeting under the best of circumstances, I want to say thank you for meeting with us today and hope we can support both you and Warren.'

Another aspect to consider when meeting with parents is how you refer to parents. A frequent complaint from parents/carers is being referred to as 'mum' and 'dad' in meetings. Some may not mind but for others it reaffirms that their identity is that of mum/dad and anything else is peripheral. At the beginning of the meeting a simple question of 'how would you like me to refer to you as … Miss …?' can help make sure you are adressing the person you are meeting with in the most appropriate fashion. Again this shouldn't be an onerous task but a quick simple way of ensuring that frustrations don't creep up in the meeting when you may, with good intention, refer to them in a way that is not appreciated.

Safeguarding

Communicating clearly goes beyond what we write and what we say. It is about establishing a culture where people are able to express concerns openly. The best schools are those that put safeguarding at the heart of what they do, and are seen as part of the wider community rather than provision that sits in isolation and only works within the school walls. It is not just about how you may conduct yourself in meetings, phone calls or how you write things down, but establishing a culture of listening to one another and engaging in successful dialogue with parents/carers, children, others in the school and external agencies.

Some things that you may say or write down will be used in a way that you don't expect as others may be taking a wider picture of events. It is important that information that you present or record about a child is clearly recorded, and accurate. If you find that information you have received is not accurate, then return back to that document, make a note of the inaccuracy, date and sign it. If it is not accurate then it runs the risks of decision-making being flawed and children not being effectively safeguarded.

In some organizations, it may not be clear what information we share with others. In understanding this we have to hold the safety of the children we work with or come across in the highest regard. But worries about what we can and cannot share should not impede decision-making about the welfare of children. In the government guidance *Working Together to Safeguard Children* it outlines that fears about sharing information must not be allowed to stand in the way of the need to promote the welfare and protect the safety of children (HM Government, 2018).

If it is a case where you do feel that what information should be shared and how it is shared is not clear, then ask and raise your concerns. Talk to a member of the senior leadership team and explain that issues around safeguarding and how you communicate effectively were not covered in the induction process. If you are feeling this way it is likely that others feel similar.

References

HM Government (2018) *Working Together to Safeguard Children*. London: DfE.

18 Managing unwanted outcomes

'When I finish school I want to be a musician' – Olivia, 15 years old
'Nah miss, I'm not going to read "Of Mice and Men".' – Si, 15 years old

This chapter is about understanding our limits as teachers or other education staff and knowing that we can do our best but sometimes the systems and processes around us mean that what we do in isolation or within a given time do not have the outcomes that we would like. I have included this in the Communicating part of the book as it recognizes that in working with vulnerable children we too may need to seek support and help when things do not go as planned or how we may expect. This chapter is a reminder to senior leaders, policymakers and other interested parties that those in education rarely have supervision, but it is something that would be likely to act as a supportive mechanism which provides a safe space for staff to reflect on their work and their responses to that work. Supervision is about a reflection on practice as well as a way to support staff in both their personal and professional development. In education, supervision has the potential to provide a space in which we can become 'unstuck' from cycles of difficult behaviour or managing those unwanted outcomes.

This chapter is given over to two children who I have never forgotten. These are two children who I wish I had done more for, in order to secure better outcomes for them. I am also using their stories as a framework to consider how we might think about our own well-being when working in challenging circumstances. Olivia and Si are a reminder that things do not always end positively, that children do not always escape and do well.

In reading their stories, I encourage you to think of children you may have worked with and still wonder about. How would you write their stories to explain what happened and what could have been different?

Bereavement

> Olivia was 16 years old when she took her own life. I met Olivia in psychiatric inpatient services when she was 14. A white British girl brought up by two middle-class parents. Olivia's mum was a teacher, her dad a solicitor.
>
> Olivia was a beautiful girl, but she didn't know it. She was shy and hid behind the top of her jumper, her eyes often peeking through. You would rarely see

the bottom of her face until you got to know her. She would speak quietly and softly and would always wear jumpers even in hot weather.

The clothes that Olivia wore hid her scars as well as her low weight. Diagnosed with anorexia nervosa, Olivia would frequently self-harm by cutting herself.

Eventually, after several months in psychiatric services, Olivia seemed to be doing better. She would smile (you even got to see this), engage in conversations with education staff, and she began to eat food in front of others and seemed brighter in mood. She would come and sit in the canteen and sit with staff while they ate. Sometimes she would even eat in front of me.

Olivia returned to school with a supportive transition programme and received her GCSE results. She began attending school from the psychiatric unit at first – a wrap-around programme of psychology and occupational therapy – and the dietician remained involved in her care as she started to move on.

But Olivia was not happy with her GCSE results, despite them being objectively good enough to go on to do A levels.

I didn't hear anything about Olivia for another year until I found out that she had taken her own life on her 16th birthday by jumping in front of a train.

Hearing the news that Olivia had killed herself was undoubtedly difficult for me as someone who had taught her, but I imagine much more so for her parents and friends who loved her and no doubt missed her every day.

In an earlier chapter, I remarked on the high mortality rate among people diagnosed with anorexia. I find anorexia an incredibly difficult psychiatric disorder to understand. It is often long lasting, and has a fundamental impact on a person's ability, from the cognitive declines due to not eating but also their approach with those around them. The drive to not eat, to be slim, to disappear from view, is one that is all-encompassing, and sadly for Olivia was something she could not escape from.

Another aspect of working with children with a diagnosis that is life-threatening (whether it is psychiatric or otherwise) is that there is a real personal risk to your own mental health. It's hard to know how it may be managed, and how to cope before things escalate into mental illness. The loss of someone who has died too early is incredibly difficult to rationalize. I would start by saying that communication is the key to managing this. This goes beyond telling friends and family how you might feel, but also means drawing upon supervision, the senior leadership team, educational welfare services and so on.

There are also other ways that you may wish to remember children like Olivia. For some it is about leaving a legacy, a moment to remember and reflect together as a wider school community. In one school that I worked with there was a community response when a child died after a seizure. It was a simple gesture of a large notebook with pictures of the child with his friends, and notes written from both his teachers and his friends. This was kept in the foyer reception for people to remember him by and as an acknowledgement from the school community that one of their members wasn't there any longer. The collective response is what becomes important – sharing your grief and sadness with others will hopefully clear a path to also be able to share your memories of the child with a smile.

The death of a loved one is particularly challenging, but this experience may be especially difficult for children and young people when they may not be expecting the death of a friend, or even if it is expected that it seems so incredibly unfair. An important part of this process of managing the death of a child is to think about how you communicate this to the children in class and in the wider school community. I encourage people to be thoughtful about the words you use to describe the death of a child. Using the word 'death' may feel uncomfortable: it is so final and clear. However, using terms such as 'loss' or 'passing', while they feel more gentle, give a sense that the child may return, and may be confusing for children.

Some children may not have the words to express how they feel. Communication does not have to be just what we say, but thoughts and feelings can be explored in a range of mediums.

Communicating with staff is another key area of managing unwanted outcomes. It is likely that your staff will need time and space to be able to explore how they feel. People grieve in different ways and may express emotions that are unexpected. Some may wish to talk about the child who has died, while others may want to carry on with their day and teach. There is no right way to grieve; there is only time that can be given for an individual to grieve in the way that is personal to them. A range of factors are likely to influence their own response to a child's death, from their own personal experiences, mental well-being and whether or not this death is reminiscent of another. In helping your staff, it is important to liaise with organizations that may be available in the local community, such as educational psychologists as well as the national organizations, some of which are referenced at the end of this chapter.

Non-attendance

A core feature of school life is children attending school on a regular basis, and there are a range of local and national targets for this. However, we know that not all children attend regularly; some may have persistence absences, truant, or as in the case of Si below, stop attending altogether.

> Si is 15 years old, mixed race with a black African-Caribbean dad and Irish mum. Si has been released from prison after serving an 18-month custodial sentence for armed robbery where he was a member of a larger gang stealing culturally significant artefacts from a museum.
>
> After his release from prison I met him for the first time; I was teaching English literature and we were studying *Of Mice and Men*. I introduced the task and he

> said, 'Nah miss, I'm not going to read *Of Mice and Men*' and sat down. He was polite, but despite my attempts to convince him he would not budge.
>
> I tried to ask him what he would like to do in the future. 'Miss, I don't need to worry about that.' After the lesson (if it can be called that), I never saw Si again. I knew that this was being followed by attendance procedures in the school and I would see his name on the register, but as the year went on, I didn't see him. As far as I know he did not move on to further education or employment.

So how do we manage this outcome? It may not feel in the same vein as Olivia's story but Si may also be at risk in terms of his own health. How do we ensure that we communicate clearly to look at addressing this issue more robustly? I think there was a naivety in my approach above, which happened nearly 20 years ago, and I would certainly approach it differently if I met the equivalent of Si now.

In communicating effectively I would start by considering the people that are involved (or should be involved) in supporting Si. It is likely to be the youth offending services and social services, but there also may be a parent who is involved in the background as well as third-sector organizations that could support Si and provide effective involvement.

References

Phoenix Education Consultancy (2020) *Helping Families Deal with Death*. Available at: https://www.phoenixgrouphq.com/bereavement (accessed 5 July 2020).

Winston's Wish website. Available at: https://www.winstonswish.org/ (accessed 5 July 2020).

19 Communicating your own needs

'If I can't help children I don't know what I am doing any more.'

This handbook has largely been given over to the needs of others: to children, young people and their wider communities. We have looked carefully at how we understand children's behaviours and how we understand and respond to the things that we notice in our classrooms. This chapter is given over to you as the reader, as well as senior leaders who may read this and be able to shape the culture of the school that you work in.

Personal self-care in the teaching profession is important, and something that isn't perhaps held in the high regard that it ought to be. There are ongoing issues with recruitment and retention of teachers, which have serious implications for the profession. The response to Covid-19 had teachers working on what was described as the 'front line' while being castigated by the media for not doing enough. The pandemic meant we lost teachers to the virus, that staff went in and worked with children who didn't understand rules relating to social distancing, that school holidays became confused with just work.

How we see ourselves may be intrinsically linked with our profession and as such it may also have a fundamental impact on our mental well-being. It is rare that a teacher goes home from school and leaves their work behind – often education staff take their work home with them at least mentally, if not actually physically carrying books to their car boot for a host of marking later on. Thus, this chapter is for you; how do you communicate your own needs and get support when you want or need it?

> In 2014, I attempted to take my own life. I didn't tell anyone what I was going to do, but I did put a post up on social media: 'If I can't help children, I don't know what to do with my life.' A person that I have never met realized the implications of this message and telephoned the police, who did a 'drive by' of a village train station near where I lived.
>
> The moment I was waiting for was missed and I went home. The police knocked on my door before I even got to my room upstairs, and they made a referral to mental health services. I had begged my GP, community mental health services and even visited accident and emergency to get some support for what I could tell was my deteriorating mental health. I felt lost and didn't have words any more to describe how I was feeling. My thoughts are normally quick and I could lose myself for hours in travel plans and enjoyment

for planning for the future. For months that was gone and I had no sense of a future. I had got rid of my bed and my mobile phone in an effort to have fewer things for my family to worry about when I was dead.

I share this story because working with children is incredibly hard work. Working with children who behave in unexpected or atypical ways can be incredibly emotive and upsetting. Feeling like you've not done enough to support those children takes its emotional toll as well. Coupling that with the stresses and strains of everyday life and potentially a work environment that may not be conducive to alleviating stress and anxieties, can be a toxic mix for your own mental health.

It is a cliche to talk about putting an oxygen mask on yourself before helping the child next to you, but one that it is worth revisiting and thinking about how we can do that practically, as well as how senior leaders in the schools and provision could help in this approach.

Beyond ourselves as individuals is the strategic oversight required to support the recruitment and retention of staff. It costs thousands to train a teacher, years at university and ongoing support in the schooling environment before they are able to teach a class independently. Yet despite this, one in five teachers anticipate leaving the classroom within two years, while a further two-fifths of teachers want to quit (Weale, 2019). The reasons for this given in the survey, conducted by a large teaching union, include workload pressure and excessive accountability. The toll is not just political; it is economic as well as personal.

So, how do we go about communicating our own needs? How do we make sure that we proactively support ourselves when we may feel judged and stigmatized by those around us?

I would start by saying that knowing yourself is incredibly important. Think about what your own signs are that you are finding things difficult; what are the signs that you potentially need to seek additional help? For myself, I am clear about what the signs of being unwell are, but they may be unnoticeable to other people who don't know me very well. I find that my thinking slows and that I can't come up with ideas in the same way as usual. I also find that my tics from Tourette's syndrome lessen considerably. I often tic when I am excited and happy, so when they diminish it can be a sign that my mood has dropped. I also find that I don't feel like I have a purpose or that my work is meaningful, and I show no interest in the things that I normally enjoy. Have a think about the things that suggest that you may need some support: what does this mean to you as an individual?

In terms of communicating your own needs, I make an active decision to do things that I enjoy. They are often things that are immediately gratifying for me, and connect me with the world around me. I incorporate mindfulness (being in the present) into things such as walks, with a particular love of castles and birdwatching. These may be ways that I escape if I'm finding things difficult, but they also feel low risk and not reliant on finances!

Another way of communicating about your own needs is about how you are comfortable with yourself. Sometimes I find that I can feel guilty that I have not worked enough (and this is very tied up in my thoughts about doing my best for the children I work with), but having time for a midday nap, or just a space to spend time with a pet, can be a real way of supporting my own mental health. Being able to communicate at these early stages is important. You may not have someone that you are able to share your early signs of needing support with, but if not make a note in your own book when you are feeling positive and the strategies you may use to support your own needs.

References

Weale, S. (2019) Fifth of teachers plan to leave profession within two years, *The Guardian*, 16 April. Available at https://www.theguardian.com/education/2019/apr/16/fifth-of-teachers-plan-to-leave-profession-within-two-years (accessed 4 July 2020).

Part V

Prevention

20 A case for prevention

We are surrounded by a wealth of research and evidence that tells us our current response to disruptive or challenging behaviour isn't working, isn't sustainable and isn't effective for many of the children we work with.

In Burstow et al.'s (2018) *Investing in a Resilient Generation*, the argument is presented that we should be looking beyond treatment of mental ill health and instead embrace a different approach that will develop the way forward to prevention. It contains a number of shocking headlines about the children we work with daily:

- Half of all mental health issues present before the age of 14 years old.
- 3 out of 4 children with a diagnosable mental health condition do not access support (Burstow et al., 2018: 8).
- Less than 1% of total NHS spending goes on children and young people's mental health (Young Minds, 2018).

Schools are in a key position where they are presented with the most difficult, enduring and challenging mental health needs in their children but aren't necessarily managing that demand. Schools, just like children, feel the effects of ACE, of abuse, domestic violence and other examples of bullying. Additionally, poor mental health is a significant factor which is associated with an increased risk of young people leaving education and a fundamental impact on future employment opportunities, and has clear financial implications (Burstow et al., 2018: 17).

There have been a variety of responses to the challenges that we currently face, all with limited efficacy. Indeed, on some occasions it is unclear if there have been attempts to assess how successful the approaches or interventions have been at all.

Some examples of where there has been an attempt to address this include the projects funded through the Alternative Provision Innovation Fund. The Department for Education gave £4 million in funding to 12 projects to look at improving outcomes for children on the roll of alternative projects. The results have yet to be finalized, but there are suggestions that there are promising results of the use of transition coaches to support children in moving on to post-16 education and the intervention of the Anna Freud Centre in providing whole-school training to schools to develop better relationships with parents in influencing change in behaviour.

In the previous chapters, I have explored some of the responses to the challenges. One such approach is 'zero tolerance' behavioural policies which are often cited as 'no excuses' and a way of maintaining the safety of staff. However, I wonder about the children on the margins of these schools – the ones where children are told that they may be better suited to a nearby school, or the children that are encouraged to use elective home education to avoid an exclusion. These children are not supported under these approaches, and while 'no excuses' sounds like a way of grounding the need for children to be responsible for their actions, there is always nuance and interplay between various factors that will put some children at a disadvantage.

The government invested in supporting schools to receive free training in supporting mental health, namely the Mental Health First Aid qualification. This qualification is set across a number of days and focuses on noticing the symptoms of mental ill health, but it is limited to a brief oversight of understanding, and responses are mainly about signposting to relevant organizations such as CYPMHS. However, at the beginning of this section, we explored how many children do not receive or have access to treatment, and that less than 1% of NHS spending goes on children's mental health (Young Minds, 2018) – with little of this spent on preventing these issues emanating in the first place.

The behaviour that we observe in school does not remain within the school gates: we know that some children may self-harm and be victims or perpetrators of violence (Harvey, 2020). This leads to an increase in demand in a range of sectors including the NHS, CYPMHS, police, social services and youth offending services. The question is what approach should we take, and it seems obvious that one where we prevent rather than just respond is the only sensible and sustainable solution.

What does prevention mean?

Prevention is the idea that we structure our approach, individually and culturally, as a way of stopping a repeat of things occurring. It requires forethought, predication and consideration of what may happen. Below are some ideas which we may incorporate into our practice to help prevent some of the behaviours that we have discussed in this book.

First and foremost, *allow children to learn in a way that causes no harm*. In other settings we might see a code of ethics that drives the behaviour of those that enter into the profession. For example, the Hippocratic Oath is a vow which outlines key features of an ethical approach. Essentially, the driving feature is 'do no harm'.

The Association for School and College Leaders outlined seven characteristics of an ethical leader. This framework saw selflessness, integrity, objectivity, accountability, openness, honesty and leadership cited as key principles (ASCL, 2019). What would it mean for educators if we made a vow to ensure that our interactions, engagement, practices and principles promised to allow children to learn in a way that causes no harm? Would that shift the way we interacted and looked at our roles as providing a service to society to help children become successful citizens?

In promoting this oath it would see us facilitating the needs of individual children, how they are different, where the similarities are and how they may learn effectively. It would also highlight the need for making reasonable adjustments for children when they (or their parents/carers on their behalf) request them. In essence it would be about working from a place of mutual respect and humanity rather than policy. For example, if a child needs to use the toilet, do they need to have a medical condition to use the toilet or could we assume that they just need to urinate? Or if a child doesn't like to be in school halls because they find them noisy and busy, can they leave the class three minutes early to avoid them without a diagnosis of anything?

What could this mean?

The above ideas are not resource-intensive but could have a fundamental impact on the children we work with. What would it mean if children didn't have to be worried about things that have a simple solution, if they knew that their views and opinions would be respected.

It would mean that children would have lower levels of stress and distress. They would know that what they had to say was valued, and adults wouldn't be in a position where they felt they had to control their bodies and actions for even basic physiological functions.

With this comes increased engagement. Of course it is important to consider our lesson planning and delivery, but when a child feels safe and secure they are not looking for the next issue or threat and can concentrate on the work they are doing, leading to an improvement in their engagement.

In not resorting to punishments such as fixed-term exclusions, permanent exclusions or internal exclusions we can tell our children at our schools: we want you to be part of our community, we want to support you, you belong and are important.

How do we do this?

If we were to personalize our approach we may find we get significant gains. This is not to suggest personalization in terms of creating a different lesson plan for each child, but just to consider the individual needs of each child. Take a moment to think about the following questions and how you could incorporate this into your delivery and engagement with the child. For example, think about the questions and relate them to the XY axis as part of your consideration:

- How do children like to receive praise (publicly, privately, with rewards, or praise or opportunity)?
- How do children like best to receive instruction – written, verbal, do they like to see examples?
- Do they like to have an opportunity to review information and then ask questions or would they rather ask questions as they go?

- What are their preferences for seating?
- When are they most effective?
- How can they most comfortably accept criticism or feedback and/or resolve conflict?

Some of these questions are the very things that underpin the planning of alternative provisions. The small scale of AP makes this more accessible to do, but also the structures around AP mean that there is often more of an individual nuanced approach to the children in those communities.

Giving children a choice over how they learn can feel worrying and even dangerous. The UK schooling system is frequently interested in control – how we make sure that children abide by certain rules that make them active and healthy citizens – but in doing this schooling systems often move towards more punitive and restrictive practices. For example, in the schooling system we control when children eat, what they eat, when they use the toilet and when they drink water. We make decisions around what they wear, how they have their hair and what is considered acceptable adornment, with little or no reference to whether or not this actually helps children learn more than those who aren't subjected to this approach.

Giving children a choice on how they learn and how they manage their bodies should be seen as a fundamental right rather than something that is earned as they age. In doing this we begin to build on doing no harm as the essence of what we do, a way of developing children who are not exposed to additional stresses that are unnecessary. We would see a reduction in children being traumatized at the end of the schooling system, children whose attendance would improve, and it would build sustainability of the economy, health service and education, and ultimately build a more resilient future generation.

References

ASCL (2019) *Framework for Ethical Leadership in Education*, ASCL website. Available at: https://www.ascl.org.uk/Help-and-Advice/Leadership-and-governance/Strategic-planning/Framework-for-ethical-leadership-in-education (accessed 16 November 2020).

Burstow, P., Newbigging, K., Tew, J. and Costello, B. (2018) *Investing in a Resilient Generation: Keys to a Mentally Prosperous Nation*. Birmingham: University of Birmingham.

Department for Education (2018) *Alternative Provision Innovation Fund*. Available at: https://www.gov.uk/government/publications/alternative-provision-innovation-fund (accessed 6 July 2020).

Harvey, G. (2020) *Increasing Knife Crime: Aggressive Adolescents or Traumatized Teenagers?*, ACAMH website. Available at: http://www.acamh.org/blog/anxiety-trauma-knife-crime/ (accessed 6 July 2020).

Young Minds (2018) *Children's Mental Health Funding: Where Is It Going?*, Young Minds website. Available at: https://youngminds.org.uk/blog/childrens-mental-health-funding-where-is-it-going/ (accessed 9 November 2020).

21 Responding: education evolution

Many new approaches to both educational and behavioural support rely on our ability to stop the education as is and restart it with a new improved design. However, it is obvious – and reiterated with the Covid-19 pandemic – that what we have now still needs to continue to serve all of our pupils and support each generation. I see the education system in the UK as needing to evolve. If we try to really understand what is working now, what the limitations of our current approaches are, and think of what could be incorporated into it, we may be able to build a new system while ensuring that the children the education system is serving now don't miss out.

We know that the education system does not work in isolation. On the local level there are a number of interfaces with a range of agencies and organizations. On the national level, politics, the economic system, families and the health system all have their part to play. Approaching eight years ago, Talcott Parsons from the functionalist school of thought saw society as having interrelated parts which influenced the whole. He described this in terms of an organic analogy, that just like brain function has an effect on the circulatory system in the body so too does the legal system have an effect on education. An evolution of the education system would have to include an evolution of the other systems in the social system.

In considering a redesign for our involved system I propose that we return to the ethical starting point: **allow children to learn in a way that causes no harm**. Develop a system that supports young people to live the unique life that benefits them, rather than follow a generic curriculum we have designed for everyone.

Accordingly, in approaching this new system, this education evolution, we then have to ask what this could look like. What could we achieve if we looked at some of the things that are working well for those marginalized children and helped the system evolve to include those things rather than children having to be excluded to access them?

First, start with the mindset of replacing concepts of zero tolerance, no excuses, isolation rooms and booths with a collaborative conversation where we ask: *How can we think of this differently? How can we solve this together?* This builds on ideas of mutual respect and transparency. It is not to say the behaviour is acceptable or to be tolerated, but puts the onus on resolution rather than punishment.

Secondly, while recognizing that many children have additional difficulties in secondary schools although they have managed better in primary schools, would an alternative solution to large-scale secondary schools be to incorporate a hub

Figure 21.1 Education evolution

Mutual respect and transparency

Hub model

Maximize use of technology

Credibility for vocational as well as academic

approach that can specialize in a range of subjects, with the associated expertise and access to resources? This would allow for a greater flexibility and personalization.

Thirdly, consider how technology can be used to support remote learning. We know that some children may not be able to access learning in school, for lots of different reasons. While for some it may be because of treatment for life-limiting and life-threatening conditions, for others remote learning may enhance the opportunities to visit hub learning, or engage in learning opportunities that wouldn't be possible otherwise (such as visits to museums or galleries internationally).

Lastly, think about the exam structure and how we view and give heightened credibility to certain traditional exams over vocational skills learning, and how we may address this mismatch in society as a whole.

It may feel that in our current approach we are so far away from this as an outcome, that it is unachievable and too far beyond what we have now, but APs are doing this every day. They are working in a smaller model to support children who have really struggled in their schools, and approaching things differently. Children have access to construction, bricklaying and hairdressing as well as English, maths and science. Some children have been physically absent from school for a year but still attend virtually through telepresence solutions, so they still learn with their friends. The Peter Jones Foundation looks at developing children's business and entrepreneurial skills and boasts that they have supported over 10,000 students to start their own business.

During Covid-19 there was amazing practice demonstrated by schools: a science teacher providing online lessons for her students, teachers using interactive learning platforms, the Oaks National Academy with teachers providing their time and resources for free.

We do not have to stick with the same model with all the limitations in its approach.

What would this mean for teachers?

An education evolution requires support and development. It starts in thinking about initial teacher training. Initial teacher training incorporates aspects relating to how to support a child's behaviour rather than manage it. Bennett (2019)

Figure 21.2 Coaching, facilitating, supporting

looks at some ways of developing teachers' practice in initial teacher training in response to concerns that teachers do not have the effective strategies required to support children's behaviour. In this document Bennett clarifies the need to use proactive and reactive measurements. In using the term 'responding' we can see how there is a need not just to act, but also to respond, reflecting on how we may prevent issues by considering the needs of the individual young people. This is not just something that we can impart and teach education staff, but is a process that requires investment and support. Instead we need to incorporate coaching, facilitating and support in the planning and development not just of teacher training, but as an ongoing process where open dialogue is welcomed.

In clinical settings there is a requirement that staff engage in supervision. I advocate the same approach in the teaching profession. Teachers are supported in being subject specialists, and rightly so, but they also need to have an in-depth understanding of how to be specialists on children and their development. It is notable that the early years stage have this as part of their statutory framework:

> Effective supervision provides support, coaching and training for the practitioner and promotes the interests of children. Supervision should foster a culture of mutual support, teamwork and continuous improvement, which encourages the confidential discussion of sensitive issues. (DfE, 2017: 21)

As the children get older, the need to promote the interests of children does not decrease; supervision would allow for ongoing encouragement for supporting not just the children teachers directly work with, but also the staff that may be working with them.

What would this all mean for behaviour?

The education evolution that I offer could have a fundamental impact on behaviour. It would help us move away from assumptive approaches to responding to children's needs. It would allow us to see that children develop from a multifactorial approach which affects a range of characteristics, as seen on the XY axis, which cannot be taken in isolation. Instead, the factors influence and affect one another and we need a more careful way of understanding this.

In changing how we provide education, there is more scope for child agency – more potential for children to assert their own responses to events rather than being subjected to an environment and relationships that are at best not helpful and at times damaging. This in turn would help children realize their own importance and value in the wider community, and reassert that while they may struggle in some areas, their opinions and views are valued. It is often seen in the phrase 'I see you' to encapsulate ideas that we observe and see a person's struggles in the wider context, and want to support them.

In developing a child's agency – recognizing their own importance in the wider community – we provide additional opportunities for success and achievement. Children will be more confident in taking risks in their learning and develop confidence and motivation. Imagine, as a child, if you were able to plan what lessons you felt were really important to you, and were able to access them; that your strengths could be capitalized in an education setting rather than something that you may be able to access out of school, if your parents have the financial and cultural resources to make this happen.

Finally, what would this mean for disruptive behaviour?

The evidence for the effectiveness of AP and PRUs is limited, and often centred on how children who attend them don't have successful outcomes in terms of education and employment figures or make progress in terms of qualifications (CSJ, 2018: 11). However, this often ignores the child's previous experience of education, and while there is an acknowledgement of previous social contexts, it is obviously difficult to map out a child's life and what might have happened if certain interventions were put in place in a timely fashion.

If we were able to support children in accessing a hub approach to education, this would also include supporting children in accessing timely interventions. If we built upon ideas associated with co-location, so professionals shared the same space to be able to meet children's needs, this would provide a better alternative to exclusions. Some of this practice is already utilized in the Family School, an AP based in London (Pears Family School, 2020). Not only is there co-location of clinicians and teachers, but the philosophy is that parents/carers attend the school as well. The purpose of this vision is a collective response to supporting children in developing more positive ways of managing behaviour that feels more troublesome and resource-intensive in the current model of mainstream education as it stands.

References

Bennett, T. (2019) *The Beginning Teacher's Behaviour Toolkit: A Summary*. London: DfE. Available at: https://www.gov.uk/government/publications/initial-teacher-training-itt-core-content-framework/thetrainee-teacher-behavioural-toolkit-a-summary (accessed 1 November 2020).

Centre for Social Justice (2018) *Providing the Alternative*. London: CSJ.
Department for Education (2017) *Statutory Framework for the Early Years Foundation Stage*. London: DfE.
Pears Family School (2020) *Our Vision and Ethos*. Available at: http://www.thefamily-schoollondon.org/about/our-vision-and-ethos/ (accessed 7 July 2020).

22 Preventing: regeneration

As this is being written, we are in the middle of a pandemic. Covid-19 has had an unparalleled impact on our lives, personally, economically, financially and educationally. In England, on 18 March 2020 Gavin Williamson the Education Secretary released a statement which said:

> After schools shut their gates on Friday afternoon, they will remain closed until further notice except for children of key workers and vulnerable children, as part of the country's ongoing response to coronavirus. (Williamson, 2020)

I read this announcement as a parent, as a teacher, as someone who works in the local authority, and wondered: what next? The whole concept of no school except for specific groups of children provoked anxiety and worry. How would my daughter manage? How would other children be supported? How will parents manage the balance of work, children and just their own mental health?

Very soon the education profession showcased the amazing things that it can do when focused on one thing – in this case, bringing education to children. Schools and colleges started using new technologies that the week earlier they had not even heard of. Those that had already embraced technology exploited this as an opportunity to make sure the more anxious children were able to access class. I know of a child with selective mutism, who refused to meet with her home tutor, but started to work independently with the Oak National Academy (an online teaching resource made by teachers in mainstream school, including videos of teachers delivering lessons, quizzes and presentations).

The pandemic caused by Covid-19 and the response from the government allowed teachers and the wider education profession to show how they can be adaptive in extraordinary circumstances. Covid-19 was a call to action, and the education professionals responded with gusto. Some examples are given below of things that showed how we could find effective and innovative ways of working in the context of the response to Covid-19.

We should see this as an opportunity to demonstrate what can be achieved if we have the focus and shared desired outcome. Throughout, this book has been peppered with stories of real children who have not had their needs met in the current education system, and for a whole range of reasons have found things difficult. With the XY frameworks we have looked at the individual nature of these children and attempted to quantify things that are relevant to us teachers. We have also used the five-stage formula to identify some issues in our class and ultimately move up through the stages to respond to them. However, this is a sticking plaster on a fundamental issue and concern that underpins the work that we are doing. To challenge this we need to:

Figure 22.1 Covid-19 regeneration study

Utilize technology

Covid-19 saw the development of The Oaks National Academy, BBC Bitesize for children to access learning, and NoIsolation's Komp to help elderly relatives who were shielding stay in touch

Adaptive

CYPMHS appointments were held over virtual platforms, mentoring using a 2-metre distance, schools turned websites into resource portals, teachers phoned children at home, meals were delivered to children's homes

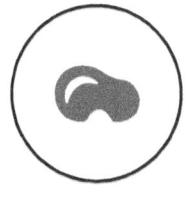

United

Schools worked across academies, trusts and local authorities. Some schools became hubs for children to learn together irrespective of where they were on roll

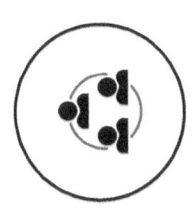

Children's voices

Organization began to produce surveys to explore children's perspectives on schooling and this began to be considered at government policy level

1 understand health (physical, mental and combination)
2 support behaviour, and
3 improve opportunities.

Understand health

In preventing the further development of children's mental ill health or distress we must get clarity surrounding the topics that have been covered in this handbook. While some of these may be characterized as mental health issues, mental illness, stress or neurodevelopmental needs, there needs to be a shared narrative that all children deserve and have a right to be in our education system. Too many children are invisible to statutory agencies, and are allowed to drift because they don't meet specific thresholds or policies, meaning that they are omitted from the dialogue altogether. We must get a clear sense of how many children this affects and gain clarity on individual implications. While the parliamentary review discussed 'forgotten children' in terms of children excluded from school, 'invisible children' are those with health needs, who are rarely discussed in the context of national education policy. While during the Covid-19 pandemic children en masse were not in formal educational provision, for many children with medical needs and some with special educational needs, there was no change at all for their everyday lives.

Once we have a knowledge of which children this affects, we must also recognize that many children will leave school with mental health and/or physical health issues. These children are likely to need ongoing support and strategies post-16 formal compulsory education. These do not necessarily have to be expensive or resource-driven, but we must hold these children in mind when looking at planning for their needs and others'.

We must understand that the many children living with mental health issues will need to make adaptations to their lifestyle, their learning and their education in order to ensure they thrive and/or survive. We must further appreciate the impact that day-to-day mental ill health and diversity can present for a child's ability to conform to the fixed rules and regulations the education system enforces, while understanding the potential damage that punishments such as isolation and exclusions can have on children in both the short and long term.

Support behaviour

Throughout this handbook we have looked at ways of supporting behaviour with the use of the five-stage formula and XY axis. In thinking about how we regenerate our approach to behaviour, I encourage you to implement the following.

Figure 22.2 Five stages of responding

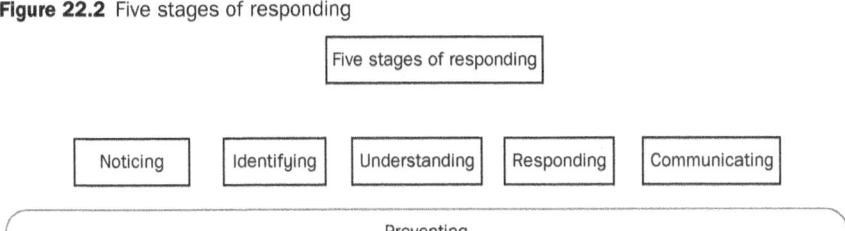

Think about your own positioning

Think about your assumptions about children's behaviour. If you are beginning with the idea that children are just bad or naughty and need correction, then I suggest you return to the earlier sections and see if that alters your own thinking around this topic. By reconsidering our own positions we may be in a more neutral place to understand and respond to the behaviour of children. When thinking about your positioning, think about your own ontological assumptions of behaviour and how that influences your interpretation of events.

Utilize the five-stage formula

If you don't feel confident in applying this formula to working with a child, think about something that you do during the day. Maybe you **notice** that you become frustrated at something, annoyed or even happy. Then move through the five stages as above to consider yourself.

Improve opportunities

The Progress 8 score refers to the average for pupils across a school, to quantify how well they progressed academically from the end of their primary school to when they complete statutory secondary education in year 11. A child's results are compared to other children who received similar results at the end of primary school. The purpose of the Progress 8 is to provide a headline accountability figure for the school (DfE, 2020: 9), with certain subjects given more weight in scoring (maths for example, and if a child takes English literature and English language). Some other subjects are not counted in Progress 8 measures. 'All full-course GCSEs count towards the Progress 8 measure, along with approved, high-value qualifications' (DfE, 2014), which include a prescribed list of vocational options (DfE, 2016). It is interesting who decides on what constitutes 'high-value qualifications', and therefore which subjects have less value. There is also an incentive for a school to offer a curriculum which maximizes opportunities for children to take qualifications that contribute to the school's Progress 8 measure, rather than necessarily what is most helpful for the individual child and their needs. If we were to conceive of a different approach to qualifications, that still maintained rigour and accountability but managed this while placing headteachers in a key position to make plans for a range of options for their schooling community, what might this mean for capitalizing on children's strengths and facilitating opportunities rather than limiting options?

References

Department for Education (2014) *Factsheet: Progress 8 Measure*. London: DfE. [Online.]
Department for Education (2016) *2016 Key Stage 4 Performance Tables: Inclusion of 14 to 16 Non-GCSE Qualifications*. London: DfE. [Online.]
Department for Education (2020) *Secondary Accountability Measures: Guide for Maintained Secondary Schools, Academies and Free Schools*. London: DfE. [Online.]
No Isolation (2019) *The Invisible Children*, No Isolation website. Available at: http://www.noisolation.com/uk/research/invisible-children/ (accessed 6 July 2020).
Oak National Academy (2020) Oak National Academy website. Available at: https://www.thenational.academy (accessed 6 July 2020).
Phoenix Education Consultancy website. Available at: https://www.phoenixeducation-consultancy.com (accessed 6 July 2020).
Williamson, G. (2020) *Schools, Colleges and Early Years Settings to Close*, Department for Education [press release]. Available at: https://www.gov.uk/government/news/schools-colleges-and-early-years-settings-to-close (accessed 6 July 2020).

Index

Page numbers in italics are figures.

absence from school
  and mental distress 67
  see also truanting
abuse
  and ACEs 18–19
  as an external home factor 11
  and insecurity 102
  and intolerance 104
  and low empathy 106
  and violence 113, 114
  see also safeguarding
adolescence 24, 54–5, 77
adverse childhood experiences (ACE) 14, 17, 18–20
agency, child 164, 168, *171*
aggression 66–7, 78
agitation 71–2, 73
Ainsworth, Mary 15–16
alcohol, foetal alcohol syndrome (FASD) 14, 17–18
alterative provision (AP) 83, 127–8, 131–2, 164, 166
Alternative Provision Innovation Fund 161
alternatives to mainstream education 127–8
anger 35–6, *35*, 36–7, *37*
  and anxiety 25
  and mental illness 73–4
  responding to 98–100, *99*
Anna Freud Centre 161
anorexia nervosa 72–4, 152
anxiety 14, 24–5
  and PDA 24
apathy 33, 40–1, *41*
  responding to 105–6, *105*
argumentativeness 78
Asperger syndrome *see* autistic spectrum conditions (ASC)
Association for School and College Leaders 162
attachment 13–16
  and nature/nurture debate 85
  and reactive attachment disorder (RAD) 14, 20–1

attention, and social learning theory 86
attention deficit hyperactivity disorder (ADHD) 14, 27–8, 54, 57–8
attention seeking 33–4, 44–5, *45*
  responding to 111–13, *111*
augmentative communication systems (ACS) 120–1
autistic spectrum conditions (ASC) 14, 22–3, 34, 55–7
avoidance
  and anxiety 25
  pathological demand (PDA) 14, 23–4, 34

Bandura, A. 85–6, 88
Beck, Aaron 36
behaviour
  defined 9
  describing *see* Phoenix Frameworks
behavioural incident reports 145–6, *146*
belonging, sense of 107–8
Bennett, T. 80, 93, 166–7
bereavement, and unwanted outcomes 151–3
bipolar disorder 77–8
Birbalsingh, Katharine 131
body language 31–2, 119–20
Boxall, Margaret 136
Broken Window theory 80
Burstow, P., *Investing in a Resilient Generation* 161

child and adolescent mental health services (CAMHS) 139
Children and Families Act (2014) 128
children and young people's mental health service (CYPMHS) 13, 139, *171*
choice, giving children 164, 168, *171*
coaching 167, *167*
cognitive contributors 14, 27–8, 54–62, 57–8
  autistic spectrum conditions (ASC) 55–7
  speech and language development 60–2
  Tourette's syndrome 58–60

communication 49, *49*, 51, 53, 119–21, 144
   face-to-face meetings 148–50
   individual safeguarding 123–6, *124*
   managing conversations 117–21
   managing unwanted outcomes 151–4
   paperwork 144–7
   telephone conversations 147–8
compulsions *see* obsessive compulsive disorder (OCD)
concentration, and foetal alcohol syndrome (FASD) 18
conduct disorder 24
confidence 38, 168
Contextual Safeguarding Network 125
conversations, managing 117–21
coprolalia 60
Covid-19 170
Crenna-Jennings, W. 138–9, 143
Curran, Andrew 54
Curtis, A. 118

death (bereavement) 151–3
defiance 33, 41–2, *42*
   responding to 107–8, *107*
delusions 71
demeanour inconsistencies 17
Department for Education (DfE)
   Alternative Provision Innovation Fund 161
   exclusions data 128
   Keeping Children Safe in Education 124
   Mental Health and Behaviour in Schools 129
   Progress 8 score 173–4
   on supervision 167
   Supporting Pupils with Medical Conditions at School 140
depression, clinical 75–7
describing behaviour, and Phoenix Frameworks 36–46
destroying work 64, 67
diaries 124, *124*
discrimination 11
disobedience *see* defiance
disorganized behaviour, and mental illness 71, 72
disorganized speech 71
disruptive behaviours
   and education evolution 168
   low-level 80
   and mental distress 66
   and mental illness 71
   persistent 130
   see also attention seeking
dissociation 109–10
distraction, and mental illness 75
distress 163, 172
   mental *see* mental distress
diversity, mental 80–3, *82*

education
   alternatives to mainstream 127–8
   behaviour in 9–12
   evolution 165–8, *166–7*
Education Policy Institute 142–3
emotional literacy support assistants (ELSA) *136*, 137
empathy 40, *41*, 105–6, *105*
encouraged behaviour 87
enforced behaviour 87
environmental factors, external/internal 10–12
ethical approach 162–3, 165
evolution, education 165–8, *166–7*
exam structure 166
exclusions 5, 128, 129–30
   and alternative provision/pupil referral units 131–2
   and fair access panels 138–9
   Forgotten Children report 93–4
   for medical needs 139–40
external agencies, communication with 147–8, 165, *171*
extreme demand avoidance disorder 24

face-to-face meetings 148–50
facial expressions 119
facilitating 167, *167*
fair access protocols 138–9
Family School (London) 168
fear 12
five stages of responding 47–53, *49*, 173
focus 89
foetal alcohol syndrome (FASD) 14, 17–18
fog friends 124, *124*
Forgotten Children report 93–4, 132, 172
formula of understanding 47–53, *49*, 173

General Data Protection Regulation (GDPR) 144

hallucinations 71
harm, causing no 162–3, 164, 165

Hartshorne, 138
hiding 19, 65, 67, 72
high-value qualifications 173
home factors, external 11–12
hope/hopelessness 12, 75–6, 114
hospital schools 132–3
hub approach 135–6, 165–6, *166*, 168
hunger 11
Hutchinson, J. 138–9, 143
hyperactivity 28
   see also attention deficit hyperactivity disorder (ADHD)
hyperarousal 19

identifying 49, *49*, 50, 51–2
identity, and defiance 107–8, *107*
impulsivity, and ADHD 27–8, 58
inattention, and ADHD 27
individual preparation 93–7
insecurity 33, 38–9, *39*
   responding to 102–3, *102*
intolerance 33, 39–40, *40*
   responding to 103–5, *104*
invisible children 172
isolation 93–4

Keeping Children Safe in Education (DfE) 124

language development 60–2
lateness 23, 53, 64, 67, 75
learned behaviour 86
lone working policies 149
looked after children 14, 17, 130

managed moves 138–9
Marino, C. 137
medical pupil referral units 132–3
meetings, face-to-face 148–50
mental distress 63–7, *65*
mental diversity 80–3, *82*
mental health 13, 129, 161, 172
Mental Health and Behaviour in Schools (DfE) 129
Mental Health First Aid qualification 162
mental illness 68–9, *69*, 172
   anorexia nervosa 72–4
   bipolar disorder 77–8
   clinical depression 75–7
   obsessive compulsive disorder (OCD) 74–5
   prevention 161

   schizophrenia 69–72
mentoring 137
Michaela Community School 131
motivation, and social learning theory 86, 88
multi-agency safeguarding hubs (MASH) 139

National Society for the Protection of Cruelty to Children (NSPCC) 125
nature/nurture debate 84–7, *85*
negative symptoms 71
neutral expressions 31
Newson, Elizabeth 23–4
non-attendance 78, 153–4
normalized behaviour 86
noticing 48–9, *49*, 50, 51
nurture groups 136, *136*

Oak National Academy 166, 170, *171*
obsessional behaviours 24
obsessive compulsive disorder (OCD) 14, 26–7, 74–5
off-rolling 142–3

paperwork 144–7
parents/carers 12, 135, 147, 148–50
Parsons, Talcott 165
pastoral care 13
pathological demand avoidance (PDA) 14, 23–4, 34
personal self-care 155–7
Peter James Foundation 166
Phoenix Frameworks 34–46, 98
Picture Exchange Communication system (PECS) 120
policies, behaviour 130–3
positive internal working models 15
post-16 support 172
post-traumatic stress disorder (PTSD) 14, 21–2
poverty 11, 18
praise 121
prevention 161–4
Progress 8 score 173–4
pupil referral units (PRUs) 131–2
   medical 132–3

Qian, X. 57

reactive attachment disorder (RAD) 14, 20–1
regeneration study 170–2, *171*

relationships 10, 12
  recognizing 84–90, *85*
remote learning 166
report writing 145
reproduction, and social learning theory 86
resolution 88–9
responding
  five stages of 47–53, *49*, 173
  individual execution 98–114
  individual preparation 93–7
retention, and social learning theory 86
reward 121
running away from class 67

sadness 12, 33, 43–4, *44*
  responding to 109–10, *109*
safeguarding
  and communication 149–50
  individual 123–6, *124*
  structural 142–3
schizophrenia 69–72
secrets, and safeguarding 125
selective mutism 14, 25–6
self-belief 10, 88
self-care, personal 155–7
self-destructive/sabotage behaviours 16
self-perception 10
self-worth 10, 11
sensory input 23, 55, 56–7
siblings 12
SLANT 131
Sobel, D. 138
social learning theory 85–6
social norms 93
Special Educational Needs and Disability Code of Practice 128–9
speech and language
  development 60–2
  support 137–8
stimulation 10
Strange Situation experiment 15–16
suicide 94, 151–3, 155–6
supervision 167
  and individually safeguarding 124, *124*
support 167, *167*
  emotional literacy support assistants (ELSA) *136*, 137
  from other adults 121
  mentoring 137
  nurture groups 136, *136*
  speech and language 137–8

Supporting Pupils with Medical Conditions at School (DfE) 140
suppression, and Tourette's syndrome 59

teachers
  relationships with 10
  roles of 13
teaching assistants 137
tearfulness 66
technology
  and Covid-19 170, *171*
  in education evolution 166, *166*
telephone conversations 147–8
telepresence robots 133
third-sector organizations 140
tics, and Tourette's syndrome 59–60
touch 49
Tourette's syndrome 58–60
transition coaches 161
trauma 16, 21, 99, 100
truanting 78, 153–4
trust 12, 89–90

understanding 47–51, *49*, 52–3
United Nation's Convention on the Rights of the Child 128
unwanted outcomes
  bereavement 151–3
  non-attendance 153–4

verbal abuse, and exclusion 130
violence 45–6, *46*
  responding to 113–14, *113*
visual communication 120–1
vocational education 166

Warnock, Mary 136
Williamson, Gavin 170
withdrawal 33, 37–8, *38*
  and mental distress 66
  and mental illness 76–7
  responding to 100–2, *100*
Working Together to Safeguard Children (HM Government) 150
written communication 120

XY axis 32–4, 139
  see also Phoenix Frameworks

zero tolerance 131, 161–2, 165